Nationalism

Key Concepts

Steve Bruce, *Fundamentalism*
Anthony Elliott, *Concepts of the Self*
John Scott, *Power*
Anthony D. Smith, *Nationalism: Theory, Ideology, History*

NATIONALISM

Theory, Ideology, History

Anthony D. Smith

polity

First published in 2001 by Polity Press in association with Blackwell Publishing Ltd

Reprinted 2003

Editorial office:
Polity Press
65 Bridge Street
Cambridge CB2 1UR, UK

Marketing and production:
Blackwell Publishing Ltd
108 Cowley Road
Oxford OX4 1JF, UK

Published in the USA by
Blackwell Publishing Inc.
350 Main Street
Malden, MA 02148, USA

ISBN 0-7456-2658-0
ISBN 0-7456-2659-9 (pbk)

A catalogue record for this book is available from the British Library and has been applied for from the Library of Congress.

Typeset in 10½ on 12 pt Sabon
by Best-set Typesetter Ltd., Hong Kong
Printed in Great Britain by TJ International, Padstow, Cornwall

This book is printed on acid-free paper.
For further information on Polity, please visit our
website:http://www.polity.co.uk

Contents

Preface

This book aims to provide a short introduction to the concept of nationalism. Its purpose is to offer students and readers a critical synthesis of much of the existing scholarship in the field, focusing on the main theoretical contributions rather than the huge corpus of empirical studies. My chief objective is to examine the various theoretical, ideological and historical facets of the concept of nationalism, and the central paradigms of explanation in the field. Inevitably, this has meant shifting the focus of attention in the later chapters from 'nationalism', understood as an ideology, movement and symbolic language, to the object of its concerns, the 'nation', understood both as a contested concept and as a form of community and institutional behaviour. In practice, the two concepts are closely related, but I believe it is important not to conflate them, especially as it is possible to discern different forms of the category of the nation prior to the appearance of the *ideology* of nationalism, and outside the area of the latter's provenance.

In a short book of this kind, I make no claims to comprehensive treatment. Inevitably, certain areas have been neglected or omitted. For the debates on such topics as liberalism and nationalism, or gender and nation, the reader is asked to consult the already large literatures in these subfields, as well as my general discussions in *Nationalism and Modernism*. Similarly, while the overall organization and tone of the book reflects my own views as an active participant in the debates on nations and nationalism, my primary concern with tracing the lines of these debates, especially in chapter 4, has meant that less space was available for developing my own views on the subject. Nevertheless, I have tried to sketch, in chapter 5, an alternative history of the nation. I hope also to have been able to convey something of the passion and complexity of the debates in the field over the last half century, while providing a clear framework for grasping the different contributions to the study of nationalism.

I should like to express my thanks to John Thompson and Polity for asking me to contribute to their series on Key Concepts in the social sciences, and to Seeta Persaud for her help in preparing the typescript. For any errors and omissions, however, as well as for the views expressed, the responsibility is entirely mine.

Anthony D. Smith
London School of Economics

The countries of Syria and Nubia, the land of Egypt,
Thou settest every man in his place
Thou suppliest their necessities:
Everyone has his food, and his time of life is reckoned.
Their tongues are separate in speech,
And their natures as well;
Their skins are distinguished,
As thou distinguishest the foreign peoples.
. . .
All foreign distant countries, thou makest their life (also)
For thou hast set a Nile in heaven,
. . .
The Nile in heaven, it is for the foreign peoples . . .

(From *The Hymn to the Aton*)

Introduction

This short book aims to introduce the concept of nationalism to readers and students for whom the field is unfamiliar.
It focuses on nationalism primarily as an ideology, but also
as a social movement and symbolic language, and explores
its meanings, varieties and sources. Inevitably, this entails a
consideration of related concepts, such as the nation, national
identity and the national state. As a result, the scope of this
work is broad and necessarily interdisciplinary: in particular,
it draws on the disciplines of history, sociology, political
science, international relations and, to a certain extent,
anthropology. The latter is included because some attention
needs to be given to the cognate field of ethnicity; for, as I
hope to show, ethnic identities and communities constitute a
large part of the historical and social background of nations
and nationalism.

The significance of this topic should not be in doubt to
anyone even mildly familiar with events since the fall of the
Berlin Wall in 1989. Few of the many international political
crises of the last decade or so have not involved a strong component of ethnic sentiment and nationalist aspiration, while
some of them – notably those in the former Yugoslavia, the
Caucasus, the Indian sub-continent and the Middle East –
have been triggered, and even defined, by such sentiments
and aspirations. These have proved to be the most bitter and
intractable conflicts, the most costly in terms of lives and

resources, the most resistant to the efforts of governments and others to accommodate the interests of the respective parties, and the most impervious to the blandishments and threats of friend and foe.

But, beyond the headlines, with their descriptions of the conflict and violence of 'hot' nationalisms, we encounter a more stable and taken-for-granted structure of 'international' relations, which shape and channel the processes and events of the modern world. This is something which is often referred to as 'a world of nations'. By such a phrase is meant not some essentialist reification of nations or nation-states, but, rather, a political map and institutional and emotional framework in and through which personalities, events and wider processes of change leave their mark and contribute to the transformations that have forged, and continue to shape, the contemporary world. Michael Billig (1995) refers to this map and framework in terms of an everyday, 'banal' nationalism, one that is habitually 'enhabited' in society – ingrained into the very texture of our lives and politics, ever-present, if barely visible, like 'unwaved flags'.

But the significance of nationalism is not confined to the world of politics. It is also cultural and intellectual, for 'the world of nations' structures our global outlooks and symbolic systems. I am not claiming for nationalism any significant degree of intellectual coherence, let alone the tradition of philosophical engagement characteristic of other modern political traditions such as liberalism or socialism. Nevertheless, even if it lacked great thinkers, nationalism – or perhaps we should say, the concept of the nation – has attracted considerable numbers of influential intellectuals – writers, artists, composers, historians, philologists, educators – who have devoted their energies to discovering and representing the identities and images of their respective nations, from Herder, Burke and Rousseau to Dostoevskii, Sibelius, Diego Rivera and Iqbal.

The cultural and psychological importance of the nation, and hence of nationalism, is even more profound. The ubiquity of nationalism, the hold it exerts over millions of people in every continent today, attests to its ability to inspire and resonate among 'the people' in ways that only religions had previously been able to encompass. This suggests the need to pay close attention to the role of symbolic elements in the language and ideology of nationalism, and to the moral, ritual and emotional aspects of the discourse and action of the nation. It is not enough to link a particular national(ist) discourse to specific political actors or social groups, let alone read off the former from the social position and characteristics of the latter. Nationalism has its own rules, rhythms and memories, which shape the interests of its bearers even more than they shape its contours, endowing them with a recognizably 'nationalist' political shape and directing them to familiar national goals.

It is these rules, rhythms and memories of nationalism with which I shall be particularly concerned here, for they provide a bridge from the outer world of power politics and social interests to the inner world of the nation and its characteristic concepts, symbols and emotions. This concern in turn shapes the way in which I have structured the argument of this book. That argument revolves around the major, underlying 'paradigms' of understanding in the field, and the political, historiographical and sociological debates which they have fuelled. These debates are diffuse and wide-ranging. They concern not only competing ideologies of nationalism, nor even just the clash of particular theories. They involve radical disagreements over definitions of key terms, widely divergent histories of the nation and rival accounts of the 'shape of things to come'.

Each of these debates and differences requires separate consideration. I start, therefore, with terms and concepts, outlining the main differences in approach to the definition of key concepts such as '*ethnie*', 'nation', 'nationalism' and 'national state', and offering my own route through this minefield. Next I consider the ideology, or ideologies, of nationalism, notably the debate between 'organic' and 'voluntarist' approaches, as well as the vexed question of a 'core doctrine' of nationalism.

Chapter 3 turns to questions of explanation, and discusses the basic divide between 'modernist' and other approaches. It then outlines the key features of the four main paradigms of explanation – modernism, primordialism, perennialism and ethno-symbolism – revealing their theoretical interrelations. Chapter 4 continues this discussion by showing how the key theoretical debates in the field over the role of ideology, rational choice, the modern state and social construction in the genesis of nations and nationalism derive from these four paradigms and reveal their respective strengths and limitations.

The fifth chapter relates different 'histories of the nation' – modern, medieval and ancient – to particular theories and their master-paradigms, and then argues for an 'ethno-symbolic' reading which links modern nations to premodern *ethnies* through myth, symbol, memory, value and tradition. A final chapter considers the prospects for nations and nationalism in a 'postmodern' epoch of ethnic revival, globalization and increasingly hybridized identity – as well as the utility of 'postmodernist' and constructionist understandings and cultural ethno-symbolic interpretations of the future of nations and nationalism.

My aim throughout is twofold: in the first place, to outline the key debates in the field as clearly as possible, and, second, to offer my own ethno-symbolic account. This is clearly no easy task. Though I outline (and defend) such an approach at various points, I am conscious of the need to give as much coverage as possible within the constraints of space to alternative theories and readings, to provide readers with the necessary information and argument to allow them to make up their own minds. Similarly, while aiming for clarity throughout, I am concerned to reveal the full extent of scholarly divisions and disagreements about the phenomena of nations and nationalism. There are no easy solutions in this much-disputed field of study, and it would be idle to pretend that we are on the verge of some general consensus. At the same time, we possess today much more information about specific cases and the role of various factors on which to base our discussions and disagreements; and that in itself allows a clearer view of the field and its problems, and hence of the tasks ahead. It is in this spirit that I offer this brief introduction for those new to the field.

1
Concepts

If there is one point on which there is agreement, it is that
the term 'nationalism' is quite modern. Its earliest recorded
use in anything like a recognizably social and political sense
goes back to the German philosopher Johann Gottfried
Herder and the French counter-revolutionary cleric, the Abbé
Augustin de Barruel at the end of the eighteenth century. It
was rarely used in the early nineteenth century; in English,
its first use, in 1836, appears to be theological, the doctrine
that certain nations are divinely elected. Thereafter, it tended
to be equated with national egotism, but usually other terms,
such as 'nationality' and 'nationalness', with the meanings of
national fervour or national individuality, were preferred.[1]

The Meanings of 'Nationalism'

It was really only during the last century that the term nationalism acquired the range of meanings that we associate with
it today. Of these usages, the most important are:

(1)   a process of formation, or growth, of nations;
(2)   a sentiment or consciousness of belonging to the nation;
(3)   a language and symbolism of the nation;
(4)   a social and political movement on behalf of the nation;

(5) a doctrine and/or ideology of the nation, both general and particular.

The first of these usages, the *process of formation* of nations, is very general and itself embraces a series of more specific processes which often form the object of national*ism* in other, narrower senses of the term. It is therefore best left for later consideration when we look at the term 'nation'.

Of the other four usages, the second, *national conscious- ness or sentiment*, needs to be carefully distinguished from the other three. They are, of course, closely related, but they do not necessarily go together. One can, for example, possess considerable national feeling in the absence of any symbol- ism, movement or even ideology on behalf of the nation. This was the predicament in which Niccolo Machiavelli found himself when his calls to Italians in the early sixteenth century to unite against the northern barbarians fell on deaf ears. On the other hand, a group could exhibit a high degree of national consciousness, but lack any overt ideology, let alone a political movement, on behalf of the nation, though it is likely to possess at least some national symbols and myths. The contrast between an organized ideological movement of nationalism, on the one hand, and a more diffuse feeling of national belonging, on the other, is sufficiently clear to allow us to treat the concept of national consciousness or sentiment separately from that of nationalism, even if in practice there is often some degree of overlap between them.[2]

The term national*ism*, therefore, will be understood here as referring to one or more of the last three usages: a lan- guage and symbolism, a sociopolitical movement and an ideology of the nation. That each of these nevertheless presupposes some measure of national feeling, certainly among the nationalists themselves, if not the designated population at large, needs to be borne in mind; for it serves to connect the more active and organized sectors to the usually much larger, more passive and fragmented segments of the population.

As a *sociopolitical movement*, nationalism does not differ, in principle, from others in terms of its organizations, activ- ities and techniques, except in one particular: its emphasis upon cultural gestation and representation. The ideologies of nationalism require an immersion in the culture of the nation – the rediscovery of its history, the revival of its vernacular language through such disciplines as philology and lexicography, the cultivation of its literature, especially drama and poetry, and the restoration of its vernacular arts and crafts, as well as its music, including native dance and folksong. This accounts for the frequent cultural and literary renascences associated with nationalist movements, and the rich variety of the cultural activities which nationalism can excite. Typically, a nationalist movement will commence not with a protest rally, declaration or armed resistance, but with the appearance of literary societies, historical research, music festivals and cultural journals – the kind of activity that Miroslav Hroch analysed as an essential first phase of the rise and spread of Eastern European nationalisms, and, we may add, of many subsequent nationalisms of colonial Africa and Asia. As a result, 'humanistic' intellectuals – historians and philologists, artists and composers, poets, novelists and film directors – tend to be disproportionately represented in nationalist movements and revivals (Argyle 1969; Hroch 1985).[3]

The *language and symbolism* of nationalism merit more attention, and their motifs will recur throughout these pages. But, despite considerable overlap with symbolism, the language or discourse of nationalism cannot be considered separately, since they are so closely tied to the ideologies of nationalism. Indeed, the key concepts of nationalism's distinctive language form intrinsic components of its core doctrine and its characteristic ideologies. I shall therefore consider this conceptual language under the heading of ideology in chapter 2.[4]

The *symbolism* of nationalism, on the other hand, shows such a degree of regularity across the globe that we may profitably extract it from its ideological framework. A national symbolism is, of course, distinguished by its all-encompassing object, the nation, but equally by the tangibility and vividness of its characteristic signs. These start with a collective proper name. For nationalists, as for the feuding families of Verona, a rose by any other name could never smell as sweet – as the recent dispute over the name of Macedonia sharply reminded us. Proper names are chosen, or retained from the past, to express the nation's distinctiveness, heroism and sense of destiny, and to resonate these qualities among the members. Similarly with national flags and anthems: their colours, shapes and patterns, and their verses and music, epitomize the special qualities of the nation and by their simple forms and rhythms aim to conjure a vivid sense of unique history and/or destiny among the designated population. It matters little that to outsiders the differences between many flags appear minimal, and that the verses of anthems reveal a limited range of themes. What counts is the potency of the meanings conveyed by such signs to the members of the nation. The fact that every nation sports a capital city, a national assembly, a national coinage, passports and frontiers, similar remembrance ceremonies for the fallen in battle, the requisite military parades and national oaths, as well as their own national academies of music, art and science, national museums and libraries, national monuments and war memorials, festivals and holidays, etc., and that lack of such symbols marks a grave national deficit, suggests that the symbolism of the nation has assumed a life of its own, one that is based on global comparisons and a drive for national salience and parity in a visual and semantic 'world of nations'. The panoply of national symbols only serves to express, represent and reinforce the boundary definition of the nation, and to unite the members inside through a common imagery of shared memories, myths and values.[5]

Of course, national symbolism, like nationalist movements, cannot be divorced from the *ideology of nationalism*, the final and main usage of the term. The ideology of nationalism serves to give force and direction to both symbols and movements. The goals of the sociopolitical movement are defined not by the activities or the personnel of the movement, but by the basic ideals and tenets of the ideology. Similarly, the characteristic symbols and language of nationalism are shaped by the role they play in explicating and evoking the ideals of the nation and furthering the goals laid down by nationalist ideology. So, it is the ideology that must supply us with an initial working definition of the term 'nationalism', for its contents are defined by the ideologies which place the nation at the centre of their concerns and purposes, and which separate it from other, adjacent ideologies (see Motyl 1999: ch. 5).

Definitions

Nationalism

The ideology of nationalism has been defined in many ways, but most of the definitions overlap and reveal common themes. The main theme, of course, is an overriding concern with the nation. Nationalism is an ideology that places the nation at the centre of its concerns and seeks to promote its well-being. But this is rather vague. We need to go further and isolate the main goals under whose headings nationalism seeks to promote the nation's well-being. These generic goals are three: national autonomy, national unity and national identity, and, for nationalists, a nation cannot survive without a sufficient degree of all three. This suggests the following working definition of nationalism: 'An ideological movement for attaining and maintaining autonomy, unity and identity for a population which some of its members deem to constitute an actual or potential "nation".'

This is a working definition based on the common elements of the ideals of self-styled nationalists, and it is therefore inductive in character. But it inevitably simplifies and extracts from the many variations in the ideals of nationalists, and assumes thereby something of a general, ideal-typical character. This definition ties the ideology to a goal-oriented movement, since as an ideology, nationalism prescribes certain kinds of action. Nevertheless, it is the core concepts of the ideology that define the goals of the movement and thereby differentiate it from other kinds of movement.

However, the close link between ideology and movement in no way limits the concept of nationalism only to movements seeking independence. The words 'and maintaining' in the definition recognize the continuing influence of nationalism in long-established, or in recently, independent nations. This is important when it comes to analysing, as John Breuilly has done, the 'renewal nationalisms' of national states and their governments (Breuilly 1993).

The definition I am proposing presupposes a concept of the 'nation', but it does not suggest that nations exist prior to 'their' nationalisms. The words 'or potential "nation"' recognize the many situations in which a small minority of nationalists who possess a general concept of the abstract 'nation' seek to create particular nations 'on the ground'. We often find nationalisms without nations – their nations – especially in the postcolonial states of Africa and Asia. Such nationalisms are not limited to the attaining of independence, or more generally, to political goals. They cover, as we shall see, important areas of culture and society; the ideal of national identity, in particular, relates to cultural issues that other ideologies neglect – and every nationalism pursues the goal of national identity in varying degrees. But, always, they come back to the ideal of the nation.[6]

Ethnie *and nation*

How then shall we define the concept of the 'nation'? This is undoubtedly the most problematic and contentious term in the field. There are some who would dispense with it altogether. Charles Tilly described it as 'one of the most puzzling and tendentious items in the political lexicon' (1975: 6), and preferred to concentrate on the state – a concept not without its problems, either. More recently, Rogers Brubaker has warned us of the dangers of reifying the concept of the nation, by seeing nations as 'substantial, enduring collectivities'. We should, he argues, rather 'think about nationalism without nations', and see 'nation as a category of practice, nationhood as an institutionalised cultural and political form, and nationness as a contingent event or happening' (1996: 21).

There are two kinds of answer to such misgivings. The first operates within the circle of nationalist ideology. On this reading, nationalism highlights the popular sentiments evoked by the idea of the nation; in this ideological discourse, the nation is a felt and lived community, a category of behaviour as much as imagination, and it is one that requires of the members certain kinds of action. Hence, its 'substance' and 'endurance', as in other kinds of community, reside in its repeated consequences, and the analyst has to take account of this felt reality through a separate concept of the nation, without seeking to reify it.[7]

The second answer touches on a wider problem. If the concept of the nation predated the ideology of nationalism, then we can no longer characterize it simply as a category of *nationalist* practice. If, further, we can envisage even a few premodern nations before the advent of nationalist ideologies in the late eighteenth century, then we shall need a definition of the concept of the nation which is independent of the ideology of nationalism, but is nevertheless consonant with it. Here lies the greatest problem, and the most insuperable divide, in the study of nationalism.[8]

Definitions of the nation range from those that stress 'objective' factors, such as language, religion and customs, territory and institutions, to those that emphasize purely 'subjective' factors, such as attitudes, perceptions and sentiments. An example that stresses 'objective' factors comes from Joseph Stalin: 'A nation is an historically constituted, stable community of people, formed on the basis of a common language, territory, economic life, and psychological make-up manifested in a common culture' (1973: 61). An example of a more 'subjective' definition of the nation comes from Benedict Anderson: 'it is an imagined political community – and imagined as both inherently limited and sovereign' (1991: 6).

These definitions undoubtedly isolate important features of the concept of the nation, yet objections can be made to both. Insofar as the 'objective' definitions are stipulative, they nearly always exclude some widely accepted cases of nations, sometimes quite intentionally. As Max Weber (1948) showed, purely 'objective' criteria of the nation – language, religion, territory and so on – always fail to include some nations. Conversely, 'subjective' definitions generally take in too large a catch of cases. Emphasizing sentiment, will, imagination and perception as criteria of the nation and national belonging makes it difficult to separate out nations from other kinds of collectivity such as regions, tribes, city-states and empires, which attract similar subjective attachments.[9]

The solution generally adopted has been to choose criteria which span the 'objective–subjective' spectrum. This strategy has yielded many interesting and useful definitions, but no scholarly consensus. Most students of the subject have, nevertheless, agreed on two points: a nation is not a state and it is not an ethnic community.

It is not a state, because the concept of the state relates to institutional activity, while that of the nation denotes a type of community. The concept of the state can be defined as a set of autonomous institutions, differentiated from other institutions, possessing a legitimate monopoly of coercion and extraction in a given territory. This is very different from the concept of the nation. Nations, as we said, are felt and lived communities whose members share a homeland and a culture.

It is not an ethnic community because, despite some overlap in that both belong to the same family of phenomena (collective cultural identities), the ethnic community usually has no political referent, and in many cases lacks a public culture and even a territorial dimension, since it is not necessary for an ethnic community to be in physical possession of its historic territory. A nation, on the other hand, must occupy a homeland of its own, at least for a long period of time, in order to constitute itself as a nation; and to aspire to nationhood and be recognized as a nation, it also needs to evolve a public culture and desire some degree of self-determination. On the other hand, it is not necessary, as we saw, for a nation to possess a sovereign state of its own, but only to have an aspiration for a measure of autonomy coupled with the physical occupation of its homeland.[10]

If in practice the line between nations and ethnic communities (or *ethnies*, to use the French term) is not clearcut, we still need to retain the conceptual distinction between them, as David Miller correctly urges. Yet his own definition of the nation (or 'nationality', as he prefers to call it) as 'a community (1) constituted by shared belief and mutual commitment, (2) extended in history, (3) active in character, (4) connected to a particular territory, and (5) marked off from other communities by its distinct public culture' (1995: 27), besides tending to the subjective end of the spectrum (it might, after all, apply to city-states and even tribal confederacies), brings the concept of the nation very close to that of the ethnic community. *Ethnies* are also constituted by shared beliefs and

Table 1.1 Attributes of *ethnies* and nations

Ethnie	Nation
Proper name	Proper name
Common myths of ancestry, etc.	Common myths
Shared memories	Shared history
Cultural differentia(e)	Common public culture
Link with homeland	Occupation of homeland
Some (elite) solidarity	Common rights and duties
	Single economy

commitment, have shared memories and continuity, engage in joint actions, and are usually connected to a particular territory, even if they do not occupy it. The only major difference is that ethnic communities generally lack public cultures. Nevertheless, Miller's definition highlights some of the main attributes of nations: the fact that they are communities, that they have shared beliefs or myths, that they have histories and that they are linked to particular territories. Can we extend this definition so as to highlight both the overlaps and the differences between nations and *ethnies*?

I propose to define the concept of nation as 'a named human community occupying a homeland, and having common myths and a shared history, a common public culture, a single economy and common rights and duties for all members'. The concept of *ethnie* can in turn be defined as 'a named human community connected to a homeland, possessing common myths of ancestry, shared memories, one or more elements of shared culture, and a measure of solidarity, at least among the elites'.[11]

While we may employ them as working definitions, these are really summaries of pure or ideal-types of 'nation' and '*ethnie*', derived from a stylization of the respective beliefs and sentiments of elite members of *ethnies* and of nations. They do not list common denominators. For this reason, they tend to highlight their distinctive elements and the key differences between them. These can be more easily grasped by setting out the attributes of both kinds of collective cultural identity, as shown in table 1.1. That ethnic communities and nations belong to the same category of phenomena is made plain by the upper half of the table: nations, like *ethnies*, share the attributes of collective names, common myths and shared memories. On the other hand, the lower half shows that nations are differentiated by their attributes of common rights and duties for members and in having a single economy. Moreover, in the ideal type, nations *occupy* the homeland, whereas ethnic communities may be only linked – symbolically – to theirs. Similarly, *ethnies* need not have a public culture, only some common cultural element – it could be language, religion, customs or shared institutions – whereas a common public culture is a key attribute of nations. In this connection, even the third attribute undergoes a change – from the various memory traditions found in *ethnies* to a codified, standardized *national history*.[12]

Nevertheless, it would be a mistake to read into this distinction any overall evolutionary sequence. After all, in the contemporary world we find many *ethnies* alongside, or within, nations, and it is at least a moot point whether some nations can be found among the many *ethnies* of premodern epochs. What can be said now, and I shall elaborate on this later, is that the ideal type of the *ethnie*, with its looser organization, is the more generic concept and the nation is the more specific; but that, in becoming more 'specialized', the nation, even in those cases where it originated from a pre-existing *ethnie*, also becomes more inclusive, more complex and less tied to its original ethnic base. The key to this paradox, as we shall see, lies in the transformation of the relationships between ethnicity and culture, and between culture and politics.

All this is rather abstract and theoretical. When we move from ideal-types to empirical instances, we find approximations and exceptions. A good example is the 'diaspora nation'. Strictly speaking, there can be no such phenomenon: a nation, as we saw, occupies its homeland, but *ethnies* may wander the earth. But, what about communities that can claim to have been nations, but which, like the Armenians and Jews, for centuries did not occupy their homelands, having lost their independent states? Can we reasonably say that they ceased to be nations, when they so clearly continued to preserve their public religious cultures and common rights and duties, and even found a new economic niche? It is a question that admits of no easy answer, and it suggests that we must use our ideal-types and the distinction between *ethnie* and nation with care.[13]

Then there are the cases of 'polyethnic nations' which comprise separate *ethnies* that have for one reason or another come together, or been forced together, and have forged a common history and shared political memories. In Belgium, Switzerland and Spain, separate *ethnies* continue to coexist within a (federal) state and their members claim both a separate ethnic and a common national identity. In the Swiss case, for example, some of the Jurassiens aspired to cantonal independence from Berne, but their aspirations were clearly bounded by a Swiss 'national identity' and political horizon. The Swiss can in general boast a definite public culture, a bounded homeland, a single economy and common rights and duties for all citizens, while even the French and Italian-speaking cantons have accepted some of the *Innenschweiz* founding myths and historical memories of the old Confederation (*Eidgenossenschaft*). More complex issues are presented in Spain and Belgium by those *ethnies* – Basques, Catalans and Flemish – that either constitute nations by the above criteria or aspire to nationhood. Can we conceive of 'nations within nations', a Flemish or a Catalan nation within a Belgian or a Spanish nation? Or is it legitimate and useful to speak of nations only within 'national states'? (see Petersen 1975; Steinberg 1976).

National state

This last is the position of those who stipulate a strictly ethnicist definition of the concept of the nation. A good example is the seminal work of Walker Connor, for whom the concepts of nation and nationalism must be sharply distinguished from those of state and patriotism. So, he would speak of a Belgian or Spanish 'patriotism' – that is, loyalty to the larger territorial state and its institutions – and contrast it with a Flemish or Catalan 'ethno-nationalism'; the latter he defines as a psychological bond of ancestral relatedness, stemming ultimately from kinship sentiments – even if the myth of

origins fails (as it so often does) to correspond to real, biological descent. By a similar logic, Connor sees a British state
patriotism coexisting with English, Scots and Welsh ethno-
nationalisms (1994: 102, 202).

I am not sure that such a sharp distinction, however useful
analytically, can be maintained. To take this last example: in
practice, the English have always found it impossible to distinguish their own English ethno-nationalism from a British
patriotism, which they conceive of equally as their 'own'.
This is not simply an imperialist reflex. Rather, it reflects the
way in which British patriotism was felt in the eighteenth and
nineteenth centuries to be a 'natural' extension of English
ethnic nationalism; and how a British nation came to be
viewed by the English, and not a few Scots ('North Britons'),
as a coming together of the various nations inhabiting a
united kingdom – despite considerable continuing resistance
to English dominance. If we recall the frequency of nationalisms without nations, does it invalidate the idea, and the
historicity, of a British nationalism (as opposed to a British
patriotism, in Connor's sense), if ultimately an integrated
British nation failed to materialize? (Kearney 1990: chs 7–8;
Colley 1992: ch. 1).[14]

Similar conceptual problems beset the French case, where
the process of integration, or at least acculturation, seems
to have gone further. Bretons, Basques, Alsatians and even
Corsicans may not aspire to independent statehood (except
for a minority), though their movements have at times
revealed a desire for some self-determination, at least in the
cultural and economic fields. But where does this leave the
French? Can a dominant French ethno-nationalism be distinguished from an equally hegemonic French state patriotism?
How can we in practice separate the French nation from
France, the national state, when so many of the key symbols
of French nationalism are political? (see Gildea 1994).

No doubt, the French example, which has been so influential in other contexts, has inspired the tendency to conflate
state and nation and has helped to popularize the notion of
the 'nation-state'. There are two problems with this com-
pound term. The first concerns the relationship between the
two components. Too often, theorists see the state as dominant, with the nation as a kind of junior partner or qualify-

ing adjective. Little attention is then given to the dynamics of
the nation. As for nationalism, it becomes a psychological
epiphenomenon, a concomitant of state sovereignty. The
second problem is empirical: in practice, as Walker Connor
pointed out some time ago, the monolithic 'nation-state' –
where state and nation are exactly coextensive, where there
is just one nation in a given state and one state for a given
nation – is rare; nearly 90 per cent of the world's states are
polyethnic, and about half of these are seriously divided by
ethnic cleavages (Connor 1972; Giddens 1985: 216–20).

In the circumstances, it might be better to opt for a more
neutral descriptive term, such as 'national state', defined as
'a state legitimated by the principles of nationalism, whose
members possess a measure of national unity and integration
(but not of cultural homogeneity)'. By making national unity
and integration a variable, such a definition avoids the
problem of 'national incongruence': the fact that the boundaries of nations and the borders of states in so many parts of
the world fail to correspond. In similar vein, we might speak
of 'state-nations', where polyethnic states aspire to nationhood and seek to turn themselves into unified (but not homogeneous) nations through measures of accommodation and
integration. This is the situation of several states in Africa
and Asia, created out of colonial territories and retaining
colonial boundaries and institutions (and often their *lingua
franca* for administrative purposes).[15]

National identity

The last term in the field of national phenomena that I want
to consider is that of 'national identity'. Its popularity is
relatively recent, and it has replaced earlier terms such
as 'national character' and, later, 'national consciousness',
which were widely used in the eighteenth, nineteenth and
early twentieth centuries. Why this should be the case is
unclear. Perhaps the present widespread concern with identity is part of a broader trend of contemporary individualism;
it may, equally, reflect the anxiety and alienation of many
people in an increasingly fragmented world (see Kemilainen
1964; Bhabha 1990: ch. 16).

Like other terms in the field, that of 'national identity' denotes both a central ideal of the ideology of nationalism, and an analytical concept. I shall return to the nationalist ideal in the next chapter. For the moment I want to suggest a working definition for a concept that is so widely used today: 'the continuous reproduction and reinterpretation of the pattern of values, symbols, memories, myths and traditions that compose the distinctive heritage of nations, and the identifications of individuals with that pattern and heritage and with its cultural elements.'

Crucial to this definition are two relationships: the first, between collective and individual levels of analysis, and the second, between continuity and change of identity. Too often, one of these components is emphasized at the expense of the other; we need to maintain the balance between them if we are to make sense of the notion of national identity.

Levels of identity We hear today a great deal about the 'situational' character of ethnic and national identities, and the prevalence in the modern world of 'multiple identities'. According to this fashionable view, we identify with a variety of collective affiliations – families, gender categories, regions, occupational groups, parties, confessions and *ethnies* – and can move from one to the other, often quite easily, as circumstances require. We can, at one and the same time, be wives or husbands, Christians or Muslims, professionals or manual workers, as well as members of particular regions and ethnic communities, invoking our membership of these collectivities for certain purposes. So, each of us has multiple identities, from the most intimate family circle to the widest circle of humanity; and, further, in a free society many of these identities become increasingly symbolic and optional (see Gans 1979; Okamura 1981; Hall 1992; Eriksen 1993).

But this is to look at collective identities only from the standpoint of the individual member. It is also possible to consider such identities as cultural collectivities, and, in some cases, communities defined by shared memories and myths, and common values and symbols. These two levels of analysis, the individual and the collective, are often confused and need to be kept distinct. While cultural collectivities and communities are composed of individual members, we cannot reduce them to a simple aggregate of individuals who share certain traits or who live together. There is so much more to these collective identities in terms of their shared values and norms, memories and symbols. Conversely, the actions and dispositions of individual members cannot be predicted from an analysis of the features of a particular community or collective identity; the latter can only tell us something about the contexts of members' dispositions and the constraints on those members. That is why it is so important to keep these two levels of analysis of collective identity separate (see Scheuch 1966).

The case is strongest where the collective identity is based primarily on cultural elements, as in the case of castes, ethnic communities, religious denominations and nations. Whereas other types of collective identity, such as classes and regions, function as interest groups and therefore dissolve more easily when they have attained their object, cultural collectivities are much more stable because the basic cultural elements from which they are constructed – memories, values, symbols, myths and traditions – tend to be more persistent and binding; they represent recurrent elements of collective continuity and difference. These elements are embodied in collective memories of great exploits and personages, values of honour, justice and the like, symbols of sacred objects, food, dress and emblems, myths of origins, liberation and chosenness, and traditions and customs, rituals and genealogies. In these cases, the collective cultural element is particularly salient and durable, and needs to be analysed separately from issues of individual identification.[16]

Hence the two parts of my proposed working definition: the first part defines the mechanisms of cultural continuity and change on the collective level, while the second focuses on the individual member's relationship to the collectivity.

Continuity and change   The above analysis may give the impression that collective cultural identities are somehow fixed or static. That is very far from being the case. True, we are dealing here with long-term constructs, but these are not essences or fixed quantities of traits. Cultural identities and communities are as much subject to processes of change and dissolution as everything else, and these changes may be gradual and cumulative, or sudden and discontinuous. The only difference from other kinds of collective identity is the generally slower rate and the longer time-span of the rhythms of cultural change, which as a result require methods of analysis over the *longue durée*.[17]

That is why the proposed definition refers to processes of 'reinterpretation' of the pattern of memories, values, symbols, myths and traditions that compose the distinctive heritage of nations. Today, we are particularly aware of how the components of national identities change, but this is a process that occurs in every generation, as external events and internal realignments of groups and power encourage new understandings of collective traditions. This process of 'ethno-symbolic reconstruction' involves the reselection, recombination and recodification of previously existing values, symbols, memories and the like, as well as the addition of new cultural elements by each generation. Thus, the 'heroic' vision of national identity, with its themes of struggle, liberation and sacrifice typical of newly independent nations or 'state-nations', may, in the next generation, cede place to a more open, pragmatic and utilitarian version of the nation's identity, stressing such themes as entrepreneurial ability, organizational skills and tolerance of diversity, themes that can be traced back to alternative ethnic traditions in the nation's history.

Hence, change is built into the definition of national identity, yet it is change that operates within clear parameters set by the culture and traditions of the nation in question and its distinctive heritage. It could not be otherwise. Insofar as identity connotes a measure of stability, of sameness over time, change can only operate within clear boundaries. Even if change is sudden and disruptive, short of total destruction of the nation, it will produce new elements that can be culturally assimilated by the membership; even revolutions tend to return to what the functionalists termed a society's 'central values'. It is the same with the transformation of nations, and it allows us to assume that the 'daily plebiscite' that constitutes the nation does in fact preserve it sufficiently for us to speak of the same nation from one generation to the next.

2
Ideologies

It is often said that nationalism has no ideology to speak of, let alone a doctrine. It is only a bundle of inchoate sentiments, elaborated by more or less florid rhetoric. Alternatively, we are told that there are too many kinds of nationalism to enable us to isolate and pin down an overall, coherent ideology. These are, at best, half-truths. Nationalism may be characterized by 'philosophical poverty and even incoherence' (Anderson 1991: 5) when compared to other ideologies. But there is more to it than mere sentiment and rhetoric, as Elie Kedourie (1960), no defender of nationalism, demonstrated through his analysis of the Herderian and Kantian philosophical assumptions of German Romantic nationalism. Nationalist ideologies have well-defined goals of collective self-rule, territorial unification and cultural identity, and often a clear political and cultural programme for achieving these ends. And, while there are certainly different kinds of nationalist ideology – religious, secular, conservative, radical, imperial, secessionist and so on – each of which needs to be analysed, they reveal common basic elements and are stamped with an identical hallmark: the singular pursuit of nationhood. These common elements mark out 'nationalism' from other kinds of movement and ideology; by isolating the common elements of the 'belief-system' that underpins the various kinds of nationalist ideologies, movements and symbolisms, we may also be able to explain some of the regularities of behaviour that we encounter in nationalist movements and 'activity'.[1]

These common elements of the nationalist belief-system are of three main kinds:

(1)   a set of basic propositions to which most nationalists adhere, and flowing from them;
(2)   some fundamental ideals which are present in every nationalism, albeit in varying degrees; and
(3)   a range of cognate concepts that give more concrete meaning to the core abstractions of nationalism.

I shall take each of these in turn.

The basic propositions of nationalism are few but far-reaching. They can be summarized as follows:

(1)   the world is divided into nations, each with its own character, history and destiny;
(2)   the nation is the sole source of political power;
(3)   loyalty to the nation overrides all other loyalties;
(4)   to be free, every individual must belong to a nation;
(5)   every nation requires full self-expression and autonomy;
(6)   global peace and justice require a world of autonomous nations. (See Kedourie 1960: 1; cf. A. D. Smith 1991: 74)

We might call this the 'core doctrine' of nationalism. It forms the basic framework of the nationalist vision of the world, and (with perhaps the exception of the last proposition) embodies the common elements in the views of the 'founding fathers' of nationalism – Rousseau, Herder, Zimmerman, Burke, Jefferson, Fichte and Mazzini – as well as of their contemporary followers. The core doctrine provides the rationale and impetus for the various kinds of nationalist activity, as well as for the symbols and institutions that express the idea of the nation. It encompasses not only the domain of politics, but those of society and culture as well; and it embraces both the cultural particularism of individual nations and the universal outlook of a 'world of nations'.[2]

Not that all nationalists have acted in consonance with the ideals inherent in this doctrine. Critics have pointed out that nationalists have often conducted themselves in such a way as to deny the basic idea, expressed in the first proposition, of a 'world of nations', suppressing the self-expression, autonomy and even the character of other nations when it suited their interests, or the alleged interests of their own nation. In so doing, they have negated and subverted the core doctrine of nationalism, which emphasizes the finite character of nations and demands an explicit recognition of the existence, individuality and rights of other, analogous nations. Hence, while in practice many nationalists have acted, as John Breuilly claims, as if their ideology related only to a single nation (their own), in theory (and sometimes in practice too, for example in Mazzini's Young Europe, consisting of several national movements like his own Young Italy, founded during the Risorgimento in the nineteenth century) they nevertheless embrace a polycentric vision of a world of finite, and *theoretically* equal, nations (Breuilly 1993; Introduction).[3]

The intellectual critique is more serious. Nationalism has often been taken to task for providing only a limited system of ideas and beliefs about politics and society, and, as a result, of resorting to force rather than persuasion in the pursuit of often unattainable goals. This was a major element in Elie Kedourie's early onslaught on nationalist ideology as a destructive, revolutionary ideology of the collective will struggling to achieve an unattainable perfection on earth; and it is echoed recently by Michael Freeden, who argues that, at best, nationalism is a 'thin-centred' ideology, with a restricted core attached to a narrow range of political concepts. This is because 'it arbitrarily severs itself from wider ideational contexts, by the deliberate removal and replacement of concepts', and therefore cannot 'offer complex ranges of argument, because many chains of ideas one would normally expect to find stretching from the general and abstract to the concrete and practical, from the core to the periphery, as well as in the reverse direction, are simply absent' (Freeden 1998: 750). Nationalist ideology is therefore structurally incapable of dealing with such major social and political issues as social justice, the distribution of resources or conflict-management. In fact, nationalism is often not a distinct ideology at all, as it simply fills out the more mainstream ideologies, such as liberalism, socialism and conservatism. The idea of nation-hood may be ubiquitous, but that may just reflect its adjacent location to many ideologies 'somewhere on the margins of significance' (ibid.). Nationalism only becomes of paramount importance ephemerally – in crises of nation-building, conquest, external threat, disputed territory, or the internal perceived dominance of a hostile ethnic or cultural group (Kedourie 1960; Freeden 1998).

Fundamental Ideals

There is some truth in these strictures, but the picture of nationalism they give is at best a partial one. The core doctrine of nationalism offers only a broad and abstract framework; it has to be filled out by all kinds of secondary concepts and particular notions, specific to each national community, such as the Swiss image of a people nurtured by its (Alpine) landscape or the Polish ideal of the nation as an embodiment of a suffering and resurrected Christ. That is why nationalism often 'inhabits' other ideologies and belief-systems, and channels their ideals and policies to nationalist ends, as happened with the 'national communisms' of the post-Stalinist era. Whether nationalism helps to 'fill out' other ideologies, or is filled out by them, is a secondary matter; it varies with the historical context. We have to go beyond the core doctrine to grasp the import of nationalism, and this yields a very different picture.[4]

There are, in fact, two kinds of response to these critiques. The first is to show that nationalism as an ideology – or, better, a belief-system – is conceptually richer than the critics allow, even if it does not match other 'mainstream' political ideologies in philosophical coherence. The second response is to argue that nationalism may be seen not only as a belief-system but also as a form of culture and species of religion; this is what makes it quite different from 'mainstream' political ideologies, and therefore largely immune to criticisms in terms of the concerns and tenets of these purely political ideologies.

Let us stay for the moment with the description of nationalism as an ideology. As we saw in the last chapter, three fundamental ideals are derived from the core doctrine, and these animate the ideological movement of nationalism: they are national autonomy, national unity and national identity. In one way or another, the more specific goals of nationalism, as an ideological movement, are variants on these three ideals, and this is why they figure in the working definition of nationalism I proposed earlier: an ideological movement that seeks to attain and maintain the autonomy, unity and identity of a human population, some of whose members deem it to constitute an actual or potential 'nation'. Let us take a closer look at the three ideals of nationalism.

The core doctrine requires that every nation has full self-expression and autonomy. The nationalist ideal of autonomy has a number of facets. In a generic sense, autonomy can mean, as the etymology implies, self-regulation, having one's own internal laws or rhythms, listening only to one's own inner voice, free of every external constraint. This leads on to the notion of self-determination advanced by German Romantic intellectuals of the early nineteenth century, of an autonomous collective 'self' seeking to realize its collective will and its individuality, and being solely responsible for its own collective goals and actions. But autonomy can also signify political freedom and collective self-rule of and by 'the people' as a result of the national self-determination of the collective will and a struggle for national self-government. Such national self-rule can be either total, in the form of a sovereign territorial state, or it can be partial, through some form of communal or federal self-government. Max Weber, indeed, argued that nations normally require their own states: 'A nation is a community of sentiment that would adequately manifest itself in a state of its own; hence, a nation is a community which normally tends to produce a state of its own' (Weber 1948).

Nevertheless, many nationalisms have had to settle for less, and some, like the Catalan movement in Spain, seem not to have wanted more than partial autonomy. Partial autonomy itself admits of different kinds and degrees, including religious and cultural self-rule, legal autonomy, economic autarchy and political 'home rule' – that is, internal self-rule within a wider state responsible for such matters as external affairs and defence. The implication here is that national autonomy must be distinguished from state sovereignty, with which it is often confused, especially in contemporary debates about the loss of national sovereignty in a European federation; and that autonomous nations may be compatible with certain kinds of federation.[5]

Autonomy is often closely linked to the idea of collective unity. This was first clearly expressed in the Jacobin ideal of *la République, une et indivisible*, and it led to the abolition of internal customs, barriers and regional institutions and cultures during the French Revolution. By creating a centralized economic and political territory and a single public culture, the *patriots* hoped to imbue all French citizens with a fervent ardour for the reborn French republican nation. But territorial unification was directed against not only internal divisions, but also external enemies, beyond the 'natural borders' of France. Other, later European nations, such as Italy, Greece and Germany, also focused on the question of borders and ethnic kin. But their nationalist drive for unity encouraged irredentist movements to 'redeem' ethnic kin as well as the 'historic' lands they inhabited which had been sundered from the national homeland by dynastic or feudal accident, by bringing them back into the bosom of the nation – by force, if necessary (see Kohn 1967b; Horowitz 1992).[6]

Territorial unity was only a first step to the much more important kind of *social and cultural* unification of the members of the nation. Such unity should not be confused with homogeneity. In contrast to the analyses of some latter-day scholars, the nationalist ideal of unity seeks not some 'objective' cultural uniformity, but a social and cultural union of families and of individual wills and sentiments. The nationalist does not require that individual members should *be* alike, only that they should *feel* an intense bond of solidarity and therefore *act* in unison on all matters of national importance. Thus, while a few, mainly German, Romantic philosophers and historians, such as Fichte and Muller, desired the absorption of the individual will in the collectivity of the national state, most nationalists have sought to unite individual desires through sentiments of love and fra-

ternity, and only *in extremis* to subordinate them to the
national will.[7]

The third ideal, of national *identity*, is perhaps the most
elusive. Generically, the concept of identity denotes sameness
in an object over time, the persistence of a specific pattern
over a finite period; and this applies to cultural identities as
well. But the ideal of *national* identity is distinguished by its
concern for collective character and its historical-cultural
basis. Rousseau had the first quality in mind, when he wrote:
'The first rule which we have to follow is that of national
character: every people has, or must have, a character; if it
lacks one, we must start by endowing it with one' (Rousseau
1915, II: 319, *Projet Corse*). And he went on to counsel both
Corsicans and Poles about how to cultivate their respective
national customs and life-styles and so preserve the collective
character of their nations. The second quality comes out in
Herder's 'cultural populism'. Each nation, he claimed, possessed, and had to follow, its own peculiar national 'genius'
– a concept that had already been popularized by writers like
Lord Shaftesbury, Vico and Montesquieu. In this vein, Herder
exhorted his fellow-Germans to return to their native cultural
traditions and literary genius: 'Let us follow our own path
. . . let all men speak well or ill of our nation, our literature,
our language: they are ours, they are ourselves, and let that
be enough' (Herder 1877–1913, cited in Berlin 1976: 182).
The implication is that to each nation there corresponds a
distinct historical culture, a singular way of thinking, acting
and communicating, which all the members share (at least
potentially) and which non-members do not and, as non-
members, cannot share. It follows that, where such a distinct
culture has been 'lost', 'forgotten' or 'submerged', it can and
must be found, remembered and brought to light. The task
of nationalists is to rediscover the unique cultural genius of
the nation and restore to a people its authentic cultural identity; as the great African writer and educator Edward Blyden
put it in respect of the African peoples:

> But the duty of every man, of every race, is to contend for its
> individuality – to keep and develop it. Therefore honour and
> love your race. Be yourselves, as God intended you to be or
> He would not have made you thus. We cannot improve upon

His plan. If you are not yourself, if you surrender your per-
sonality, you have nothing left to give the world. You have no
pleasure, no use, nothing that will attract and charm men, for
by suppression of your individuality you lose your distinctive
character. (Blyden 1893, cited in Wilson 1969: 250)

This emphasis upon national individuality helps to explain
why nationalisms are so often accompanied and fuelled by
the labours of intellectuals intent on tracing the 'roots' and
'character' of the nation through such disciplines as history,
archaeology, anthropology, sociology, linguistics and folklore. These scholarly disciplines provide the tools and conceptual frameworks for finding out 'who we are', 'when we
began', 'how we grew' and perhaps 'where we are going';
just as the Romantic artists and writers, journalists and
educators, such as Blyden, help to convey and disseminate the
images and representations of national identity.[8]

Of course, in particular nationalisms and specific historical moments, one or other of these three ideals will attain
greater prominence. Where the actual or potential nation
lacks a measure of autonomy, or is felt to be disunited, or
fails to project a clear identity profile, nationalists will
attempt to remedy the situation by measures to attain or
renew national autonomy, unity or identity. But, in general
and over the course of time, we can expect to find ideological movements of nationalism seeking to achieve the fullest
expression of all three national ideals.

Core Concepts

These ideals of autonomy, unity and identity remain at a high
level of abstraction, and they require other core concepts to
relate them to practical cultural and political programmes.
The most important are those of authenticity, continuity,
dignity, destiny, attachment ('love') and the homeland, all of
which provide criteria for the evaluation of past and present
states of the nation, and for attaining its desirable goals,
though not all may be invoked by specific nationalisms –
which may become a cause of incomprehension and, ultimately, conflict (see Gilbert 1998; ch. 1).

Nations, as we have seen, to be free, need to express themselves. But what exactly is the 'self'? For the nationalist, the
only answer is to be found in the concept of *authenticity*. To
be 'truly' ourselves, means to find the 'authentic' elements of
our being, and strip away the accretions of the ages. Thus,
historians of the German school of history led by Leopold
von Ranke in the nineteenth century sought to uncover an
authentic past as it actually was (*wie es eigentlich war*);
modern musicologists aim to play early music in authentic
style and with authentic period instruments; and modern
archaeologists and art historians seek to authenticate ancient
objects or Old Masters. Here, authenticity translates into correspondence with 'truth', opposing the genuine to the fake,
but also into what was the original version of an object, style
or way of life. This leads on imperceptibly to the notion of
authenticity as originality and, in the nationalist context, to
a myth of origins and descent: 'who we are' is a function of
'whence we came' in time and space; character is determined
by origin. But this overlaps with yet another meaning: the
idea of being originary and indigenous, that is, not only the
first of its kind but also autochthonous, sprung from the soil.
That in turn leads on to another sense of the authentic as
pure and unmixed, where the genuine 'we' constitute a pristine original, however mixed our present lamentable state.
But perhaps the most common sense in which nationalists use
the adjective 'authentic' is to denote what is 'our very own'
and nobody else's, and hence unique, but equally inner-
determined. Here, the concept of authenticity overlaps with
that of autonomy: the 'true' community is also the self-
determining nation.[9]

All these meanings are used by nationalists, often quite sin-
cerely, and the problem is not one of conceptual poverty so
much as conceptual ambiguity. Similar problems beset other
nationalist concepts. Take the notion of *continuity*. It can
denote something akin to the generic concept of identity,
sameness over time, hence the idea of the unchanging nation
beneath all the ravages of time, awaiting its moment of regeneration. But it can also signify a gradual movement of change
and transformation, or an accumulation of layers of past
states, like the strata of an archaeological excavation. In these
evolutionary models, continuity is not opposed to change;

rather, change is continuous, and continuity, the continuity of growth, is always imperceptibly changing. Here, the very term lends itself to ambiguity, something that nationalists have both keenly felt and known how to exploit.[10]

The notion of national *dignity*, too, is not as straightforward as it might appear. Present humiliation and oppression is opposed to the dignity which liberation will bring, but it does not, of itself, produce the desire for dignity. This must be 'rediscovered' within. Hence the second meaning: dignity as 'true worth', concealed by external disfigurements. The goal is to find that inner worth, to realize the dignity of the authentic self. This was sometimes expressed in the Asian phrase 'Western arts, Eastern morality', implying the innate spiritual superiority of Asia, despite Western technological prowess. Such a stance safeguards the inner dignity of the humiliated, and promises a status reversal in which the oppressed and peripheralized will be restored to their former greatness, and external status will mirror inner worth – the sentiment of the leaders of Meiji Japan. Dignity can also come from noble pedigree and antiquity, which attract reverence and piety. The quest for collective dignity elevates the 'true' national self through comparisons with the degradations of its present state and with unworthy outsiders. This is particularly the case where a well-documented heroic or 'golden' age provides a standard for evaluating the communal present.[11]

The nation, in the eyes of nationalists, can be described as a community of history and destiny, or better, a community in which history requires and produces destiny – a particular national destiny. This idea of *destiny* carries far more emotional freight than notions of the future. Destinies are predetermined by histories; destinies chart a unique course and fate; destinies speak of transcendence, perhaps immortality; for we 'live on' in the memory and judgement of posterity. For nationalists, the nation's destiny is always glorious, like its distant past; indeed, the golden past, hidden beneath the oppressive present, will shine forth once again, through the regeneration of the true spirit of the nation by the yet unborn. So the destiny of each nation is not to return to the glorious past, but to recreate its spirit in modern terms and under transformed conditions (see Anderson 1999).

Equally important for nationalists is the ideal of conscious *attachment* to the nation. Such consciously desired sentiment is not peculiar to nationalism; Pericles, after all, in the memorable phrase of Thucydides, enjoined his fellow-citizens of Athens to 'fall in love with their city', and we can find examples of exhortations to attachment, love and self-sacrifice, in both civic and religious contexts. But nationalism has elevated this conscious collective attachment to a pre-eminent position. 'Love of the nation' is its supreme political virtue. Hence, all those appeals to the members of a great 'family', for the defence of 'kith and kin' and 'hearth and home', and the need for self-sacrifice for the good of 'our country'. As Michel Aflaq, the co-founder of the Syrian Ba'ath (Resurrection) Party in the 1950s, put it: 'Nationalism is love'. This is that abstract love, said Kedourie, that has fed the greatest acts of terror (see Binder 1964; Kedourie 1971: Introduction).[12]

Political 'love' gives palpable expression to the abstraction of the nation. It is, after all, love of one great family. But 'family' and 'home' go together in popular imagination, and love demands that families have homes; homeless families need political roofs; a nation without a 'homeland' is a pariah people. So, 'attachment' and the *'homeland'* reinforce each other in a quest for a return to roots. Even nations that reside in their homelands need 're-rooting', reattaching themselves to their pristine origins, their authentic self. This is just one of the many meanings of the concept of the homeland.

The concept of the homeland may also act as a title-deed, a political claim to a specified area of land and its resources, often in the teeth of opposition from rival claimants. From this perspective, the homeland is indispensable for economic well-being and physical security; and the exploitation of its agricultural and mineral resources becomes a prime nationalist consideration. This is one reason for the nationalist drive for economic self-sufficiency, or at least self-sustaining growth. It may also help to explain the nationalist agrarian idyll, its emotional attachment to the 'folk' and the life-style and customs of the peasantry, while in practice nationalisms often relentlessly pursue policies of rapid industrialization.[13]

On another level, the homeland constitutes an historic territory, the ancestral land. It is the land of our forefathers and foremothers, and contains their last resting-places. It is also the arena and indispensable setting for the great men and women, and the turning points, in the nation's history – battles and treaties, synods and assemblies, the exploits of heroes and the shrines and schools of saints and sages. Then there is the landscape itself. What nationalism does not extol the peculiar beauty of 'our' hills and mountains, our rivers, lakes and fields, whom the deity (or deities) has blessed? We can hardly begin to enter into the world-view of nationalism without appreciating the profound effects of these 'poetic landscapes' on the self-understanding of many members of the nation, nationalist and non-nationalist alike – an aspect that has till recently been rather neglected, and one to which I shall return.[14]

I do not wish to claim that all of these concepts are invoked by every nationalist ideology or movement, and certainly not to the same degree. That is clearly not the case. Paul Gilbert correctly argues that some of the disputes between rival nationalisms turn on their invoking different, and competing, core concepts of the nation – for example, a nationalism invoking a concept of the nation based on territory and the homeland versus one based on ethnicity and culture. But, while the historical record is replete with such conflicts, I am not sure that his answer to the question as to why the participants (and we) should classify all of them as 'nationalisms' is adequate. Taking his cue from Weber, Gilbert claims that they share what he calls the 'constitutive principle of nationalism' which holds that nations are groups that have a right to national self-determination, which in turn may well involve 'a national right to independent statehood'; and further, that nations 'are the kind of group that has this right' (1998: 16). But, not all nationalists make this claim. Cultural nationalists, for example, argue that nations have the right to cultural autonomy and moral regeneration that falls well short of statehood; they may not even consider that it is desirable that their (or any) nation should become independent and have a state of its own. More generally, the claim to statehood is just one, albeit an important, goal of many nationalisms, along with other goals, such as national unification and identity (see Hutchinson 1994: ch. 1).

In fact, it might be better to view nationalist ideologies as examples of a family of overlapping concepts of 'nationalism'

of the kind I have discussed, similar to the generic concept
of a 'game' which has several overlapping elements, not
all of which appear in each and every type of game; except
that perhaps, in all of these nationalist ideologies, we can
discern the three broad goals of national identity, unity and
autonomy, albeit in varying degrees. On this reading, the core
concepts shape the general world-view of nationalist ideologies and the political programmes derived from them; but different combinations of these concepts point them in different
directions, creating the various kinds of nationalism with
which we are familiar. Now, while these ideologies do not,
and cannot, embrace all the issues and questions which other
political ideologies encompass, they are conceptually far
richer than the critics imply and they address a wide range
of problems, needs and preoccupations that these other
'mainstream' political ideologies often ignore, to their cost.
Besides, there is, as Kedourie argued, little point in using 'the
categories of one ideology to test and classify the tenets of a
completely different ideology' (Kedourie 1960: 90). If nationalisms fail to address questions of social justice or the distribution of resources, except in a very indirect and vague
manner, it is because their sights are set on the ideals and
problems of identity, autonomy, unity and authenticity which
these other ideologies hardly touch on.

Nationalism as Culture and Religion

The second response to the critics' strictures is to show that
nationalism is much more than a political ideology; it is also
a form of culture and 'religion'. This line of reply brings into
focus the central concept of nationalism, that of the 'nation'.

The nationalist conception of the nation is not, of course,
monolithic, and I shall be exploring some of its ideological
variants later. Nevertheless, all the variants agree in regarding the nation as a form of *public culture*, open in principle
to all members of the community, or all the citizens of the
'national state'. As we saw, nationalism demands the rediscovery and restoration of the nation's unique cultural identity; and this means returning to one's authentic roots in the

historic culture community inhabiting its ancestral homeland. As a form of culture, the nation of the nationalists is one whose members are conscious of their cultural unity and national history, and are devoted to cultivating their national individuality in vernacular languages, customs, arts and landscapes, through national education and institutions. To quote Rousseau again:

> Ce sont les institutions nationales qui forment le génie, le caractère, les goûts et les moeurs d'un peuple . . . qui lui inspirent cet ardent amour de la patrie. (It is the national institutions that form the genius, the character, the tastes and the mores of a people . . . which inspire in it this ardent love of the fatherland.) (Rousseau 1915, II: 431, *Considérations sur le gouvernement de la Pologne*)

For the nationalist, what is indigenous is ipso facto popular; we must therefore rediscover the culture of 'the people' through popular education and instil a national love of the people. Hence the oft-noted strong populist and romantic elements in most nationalisms (Nairn 1977: ch. 2).[15]

But this popular, national culture is not just a private affair. The nation's culture demands public expression and gives birth to a political symbolism. The return to an authentic history and a vernacular culture must take a public form and be politicized. The cultural nation must become the political nation, with public culture the mould and measure of society and polity. The nation is therefore characterized by a 'political culture', with its distinct political roles and institutions and its unique symbols – flags, anthems, festivals, ceremonies and the like.

Where the nation in question emerged on the basis of prior ethnic ties, vernacular forms of culture permeate its public life and identify its political culture, as in Poland. Where the nation is polyethnic and claims to possess a more 'civic' character, some of the cultural forms may be borrowed, as in India, though at some cost to national unity. In other cases, like France, where an ancestral culture underlies a civic conception of the nation and a territorial nationalism, vernacular cultural codes may coexist uneasily with a more universal republican symbolism.

Despite these variations, the overall thrust of nationalism is clear: the nation is a form of public culture and political symbolism, and ultimately of politicized mass culture, one which seeks to mobilize the citizens to love their nation, observe its laws and defend their homeland.

Yet there is more to nationalism than secular culture. However secularizing its thrust, nationalism is ultimately more akin to 'political religion' than to political ideology. Here I am using the Durkheimian definition of religion as 'a unified system of beliefs and practices relative to sacred things, that is to say, things set apart and forbidden – beliefs and practices which unite into one single moral community called a Church, all those who adhere to them' (Durkheim 1915: 47). This functional approach is useful for understanding the surrogate religion of nationalism, as is Durkheim's own emphasis on the role of the sacred and of ritual. This is very evident in the importance conferred by nationalism on commemorative ceremonies for great leaders or for the fallen in battle, the 'glorious dead' who sacrificed their lives for their country. At such moments, we can grasp the nation as a 'sacred communion of citizens' – a characterization that accords with an interpretation of nationalism as 'surrogate religion'.[16]

There are other aspects of nationalism which reveal its character of surrogate political religion. Time and again, we encounter the self-image of an elect nation, a unique people with a peculiar history and destiny, the secular successor to older religious beliefs in ethnic election, or the 'chosen people'. These are self-images that can be found in nations as far apart as France and Japan, India and the United States. Then there is the quasi-messianic fervour which attaches to their founders and leaders. In the new states of Africa and Asia, the men who led their nations to independence – such as Nehru and Sukarno, Nkrumah and Kenyatta – acquired almost sacred status at the time as prophets and saviours of their people, ushering in a new era of freedom, justice and love. Even more important are the twin beliefs in national destiny and ethnic posterity, as described earlier. These beliefs supplement and sometimes supplant traditional religious faith in an after-life, which they transfer to an earthly plane, with a promise of collective immortality carried in and through the yet unborn generations of the nation (see A. D. Smith 1999a: chs 3, 9).

All this tells us something about the complexity of nation-alism. Appearing as a political ideology on one level, it reveals itself on other levels as a form of public culture and a surro-gate political religion. It is therefore misleading to seek to compare nationalism *tout court* with other 'mainstream' political ideologies, even within the West, their home and main arena. Nationalism needs to be understood as a global phenomenon with several facets, and it is important to explore each of these if we are to grasp so protean a phenomenon.

Voluntarism and Organicism

So far I have treated the ideologies of nationalism in a fairly undifferentiated manner. I have sought to stress common tenets, shared ideals and core concepts. But, as I indicated, this is to overlook some fairly systematic differences between nationalisms which suggest the need for a typology of the basic forms of nationalist ideology. The most familiar typ-ology is also the simplest and most far-reaching: I refer to the 'voluntarist' and the 'organic' kinds of nationalism, which have had the longest history and the most dramatic consequences.[17]

The *locus classicus* for the debate about the two kinds of nationalist ideology can be found in Ernest Renan's critique of Heinrich von Treitschke in his 1882 lecture, entitled *Qu'est-ce qu'une nation?* Whereas Treitschke employed an ethno-linguistic criterion to legitimate the German annexa-tion of the disputed territories of Alsace and Lorraine, claim-ing that despite their clearly expressed political will and historical memories, the Alsatians were 'objectively' ethnic Germans, Renan argued for a more political, and to a certain extent voluntary, approach. While conceding something to the 'Germanist' thesis of the origins of France, insofar as the Germanic (Frankish) tribes brought monarchical government and lasting territorial divisions to Western Europe, he never-theless affirmed the spiritual nature of nations and the importance of historical memories and political will. Against ethnic determinism, Renan affirms the primacy of 'human culture' over particular national cultures, and the need for 'consent, the clearly expressed desire to continue a common life. A nation's existence is, if you will pardon the metaphor, a daily plebiscite, just as the individual's existence is a perpetual affirmation of life' (Renan 1882, cited in Bhabha 1990: 19). This well-known passage is often taken out of context to demonstrate a liberal and voluntarist ideal of nationality, in contrast to the organicism and determinism of German Romantic ideology. To be sure, Renan eschews both determinism and the organic analogy, but it is not to assert a doctrine of voluntary nationality or the individual's right to choose her or his nation. Rather, he seeks to vindicate an historical and an activist political understanding of the nation, one that would give due weight to the 'cult of the ancestors' and to a 'heroic past'. The analogy of the nation with the individual is not intended to support a liberal theory of individual preferences or a situational analysis of group identities. It is used to confirm the role of the past, of history and memory (and forgetting), as well as of continuing political will, in forging nations:

> The nation, like the individual, is the culmination of a long past of endeavours, sacrifice and devotion. Of all cults, that of the ancestors is most legitimate, for the ancestors have made us what we are. A heroic past, great men, glory (by which I understand genuine glory), this is the social capital upon which one bases a national idea. To have common glories in the past and to have a common will in the present; to have performed great deeds together, to wish to perform still more – these are the essential conditions for being a people. (Ibid.: 19)

Max Weber, German nationalist though he was, came to a similar conclusion. He, too, insisted on the role of historical memory and political will. On his visit to the museum in Colmar, he reported that:

> The reason for the Alsatians not feeling themselves as belonging to the German nation has to be sought in their memories. Their political destiny has taken its course outside the German

sphere for too long; for their heroes are the heroes of French history. If the custodian of the Colmar museum wants to show you which among his treasures he cherishes most, he takes you away from Grunwald's altar to a room filled with tri-colors, *pompier*, and other helmets and souvenirs of a seem-ingly most insignificant nature; they are from a time that to him is a heroic age. (Weber 1948: 176)

He goes on to note the Alsatians' sense of French community and their attachment to these relics, 'and especially memora-bilia from the French Revolution'. This sense of community, he writes, 'came into being by virtue of common political and, indirectly, social experiences which are highly valued by the masses as symbols of the destruction of feudalism, and the story of these events takes the place of the heroic legends of primitive peoples' (Weber 1968, I: 396).

Weber's general position on nations and nationalism, though never fully articulated, was, in one sense, closer to Renan, in that he stressed the importance of political action and institutions, along with historical memories. But it was also still greatly influenced by the ethno-linguistic criteria of nationality which had for a century been central to the German Romantic tradition. That tradition had drawn its inspiration from Herder and Kant, and further back from Rousseau's 'naturalism', the belief that nations must be conceived, as Siéyès, the French political philosopher and statesman of the late eighteenth century put it, 'in the state of nature' – though the legislator may make up that which is defective in nature. Similarly, early nineteenth-century German Romantics such as Fichte, Arndt and Jahn were convinced of the underlying naturalness of (ethno-linguistic) nations, but they combined this belief with a firm commit-ment to state education in order to inculcate a correct national will and the need for struggle to achieve true freedom and to exercise genuine national self-determination (see Kedourie 1960: ch. 3).

For the Romantics, as for Renan, the nation was a spiri-tual principle, a 'national spirit' (*Volksgeist*), and each nation had its peculiar destiny and mission, as well as its unique culture, the 'irreplaceable culture values', belief in which Weber saw as the hallmark of nationalism. But, unlike Renan, the German Romantics discovered the source of the national spirit, not in history or politics, but in 'culture-made-will', in the organic linguistic culture expressed through the exercise of national will in the quest for self-realization in statehood. This criterion of the national spirit reflected the history and contemporary situation of the German-speaking territories, divided as they were until 1871 into many kingdoms and principalities, whose only commonalty lay in the German language and literature. Though some German Romantics appealed to a common history – the concept of Germania had been popular among the German-speaking Renaissance humanists and the later Holy Roman Empire had increasingly centred on the German-speaking territories – language and ethnicity quickly came to exert a greater appeal, first against the external enemy, French culture, and later increasingly against the internal Jewish 'racial enemy'. This uncertainty over core values and the efficacy of cultural bonds, coupled with a growing fear of cultural and ethnic pollution from within, influenced the course of German nationalist ideologies in the direction of an ethnic nationalism and a biological determinism, but more generally such a cultural nexus has encouraged the trend towards more naturalistic and organic ideologies of the nation (see Mosse 1964; Kohn 1965; Conversi 1997).[18]

'Ethnic' and 'Civic' Nationalisms

Contemplation of the course of German nationalism, in particular, was an important factor in the development of Hans Kohn's dichotomy of 'Western' and 'Eastern' nationalisms, still the most celebrated and influential of the typologies of nationalism. Hans Kohn's major work, *The Idea of Nationalism*, appeared in 1944. Written in the shadow of Nazism and the war, it sought to uncover the differences, as Kohn saw it, between the more benign forms of nationalism found in the West and the more virulent varieties that had appeared east of the Rhine. Kohn argued that Western forms of nationalism were based on the idea that the nation was a rational association of citizens bound by common laws and a shared territory, whereas Eastern varieties were based on a belief in common culture and ethnic origins, and as such tended to regard the nation as an organic, seamless whole, transcending the individual members, and stamping them from birth with an indelible national character. Sociologically, the source of this contrast was to be found in their different class formations. In the West, a strong, confident bourgeoisie was able to build a mass citizen-nation with a civic spirit; whereas the East, lacking such a bourgeois class, and ruled by imperial autocrats and semi-feudal landowners, provided fertile soil for organic conceptions of the nation and for shrill, authoritarian and often mystical forms of nationalism (Kohn 1967a).

Despite the many criticisms levelled at Kohn's dichotomy – its moralistic exaggeration of the distinction, its geographical focus which overlooked important 'exceptions' such as Ireland and the Czechs, and its oversharp delineation of the two types – it retains an important kernel of truth. In the 'voluntarist' conception of the nation, individuals have some latitude; although they must belong to a nation in a 'world of nations' and national states, they can, in principle, choose to which nation they wish to belong. In the 'organic' conception, no such choice is possible. Individuals are born into a nation, and wherever they may migrate, they remain an intrinsic part of their nation of birth.[19]

This is, of course, an ideological criterion and it describes normative types. There have been attempts to create more historical and sociological distinctions, from the work of Carlton Hayes and Louis Snyder to later formulations such as Hugh Seton-Watson's distinction between the 'old, continuous nations' of (mainly) Western Europe and the new, deliberately created nations ('nations of design', as Charles Tilly described them) of Eastern Europe and Asia, and my own distinction between nationalisms based on 'territory' and those based on 'ethnicity'. These typologies may well sensitize us to important differences between nations and nationalisms, but the problem is that so many nationalisms change 'character' over time and so often partake of elements of both types, that the original analytic distinction loses much of its practical value.[20]

Besides, there is the danger of importing normative judgements into sociological types. This is the problem with the currently fashionable distinction between 'ethnic' and 'civic' conceptions of the nation. While civic nationalism *may*, in the eyes of some political philosophers, be combined with liberalism and so achieve a measure of respectability, ethnic 'blood-and-soil' forms of nationalism remain beyond the moral pale; their unregenerate particularism debars them from any civilized intercourse with 'mainstream' political ideologies. It may be possible to provide a liberal rationale for giving prior attention to the needs of co-nationals, provided this rationale is based on residence, history and public culture, not on genealogy and ethno-linguistic culture. This is very much in line with David Miller's definition of the concept of the nation; its list of components include history, territory and public culture, but omits all reference to myths of ethnic descent. And the same holds for Maurizio Viroli's defence of republican patriotism against the claims of (German Romantic) ethno-cultural nationalism (Miller 1995; Viroli 1995; cf. Barry 1999).

But even such a pared down version of nationalism may produce quite illiberal, xenophobic policies. The classic example from the 'home' of civic nationalism was the French Republic's treatment of the Jews in their midst. 'To the Jew as individual we give everything, to the Jew as Jew nothing', declared Clermont-Tonnerre in the French Assembly in 1790. Civic nationalism's failure to endorse minority group rights may be consonant with liberal individualism and individual human rights, but only by conveniently overlooking the group rights accorded to the majority (host) nation. These rights or duties included the necessity for citizens to learn and conduct affairs in the dominant (French) language, to learn and recite the majority (French) history and literature, to observe French customs, to recognize French political symbols and institutions, and so on. For the Jews, this meant splitting their unitary self-concept and their ethno-religious community into a religious confession and an ethnic affiliation, stripping them of the latter, and assimilating them into the host nation – a procedure applied by liberal civic nationalism to minorities in many national states to this day (see Vital 1990: ch. 1; Preece 1998).

Civic nationalism, then, is very far from accommodating the group claims of different cultures. A genuine multiculturalism can only exist in the framework of a 'plural' nation, which celebrates diversity and includes its different component cultures within the overarching political institutions and symbols of the national state. This became very much the case in the United States of America only after the abandonment of the melting-pot ideology in the late 1960s. Though the United States was, in fact, built on the cultural base of a Protestant English *ethnie*, slavery, conquest of the Native Americans and successive waves of immigration have turned it into a truly polyethnic and plural nation, yet one bound by a common language, common laws, shared political symbols and a 'secular religion' – saluting the flag, celebrating public holidays, the cult of the Constitution and the founding fathers, commemorations of the glorious war dead, and so on.

Yet, for all the apparent differences, the similarities between the providential nationalism of the United States and the 'missionary' nationalisms of France, Russia and Britain – 'great nations', 'beacons of progress' and 'bearers of civilization' to 'ignorant natives' – are much more striking. They confirm that, despite the evident contrasts between 'organic' and 'voluntarist' types of nationalist ideology, and the 'ethnic' and 'civic' conceptions of the nation, there is greater affinity between the policies they inspire than one might have been led to expect. This means that, in conducting causal analysis, we need to treat nationalism as a single set of phenomena, while bearing in mind the ideological differences between its various forms. The basic tenets, ideals and core concepts of nationalism have remained fairly constant through time and across cultures; and this helps to explain why, despite the failure to agree common definitions of terms and a common explanatory paradigm, scholars have felt able to propose all-embracing explanations of nations and nationalism, and rival nationalists have been able to engage in debate with each other.

3
Paradigms

In early 1789, the Abbé Siéyès published a pamphlet, entitled *Qu'est-ce que le Tiers Etat?*, in which he attacked the privileges of the nobility and clergy, identified the Third Estate with the nation, and proclaimed the sovereignty of the nation:

> The Nation exists before all things and is the origin of all. Its will is always legal, it is the law itself . . . Nations on earth must be conceived as individuals outside the social bond, or as is said, in the state of nature. The exercise of their will is free and independent of all civil forms. Existing only in the natural order, their will, to have its full effect, only needs to possess the *natural* characteristics of a will. In whatever manner a nation wills, it suffices that it does will; all forms are valid and its will is always the supreme law. (cited in Cobban 1963, I: 165; italics in original)

The *Declaration of the Rights of Man and the Citizen* later that year put the matter even more succinctly: 'The source of all sovereignty resides essentially in the Nation: no body of men, no individual, can exercise authority that does not emanate expressly from it' (see Baker 1988: 271). A year later, in the summer of 1790, French men and women celebrated the *Fête de la Fédération*: national guardsmen and loyal citizens came together to celebrate the new French federation. Everywhere, altars were erected with the inscription:

'The citizen is born, lives and dies for the fatherland.' Processions were held, hymns sung and oaths sworn, with outstretched interlinked arms, in imitation of Jacques-Louis David's painting *The Oath of the Horatii* (1784). Embracing in 'holy fraternity', the citizens swore everlasting allegiance to France, to uphold her national unity and obey the sovereign people. In Paris, on 14 July, on the Champs de Mars, LaFayette administered the oath and Talleyrand provided a mass and benediction under streaming flags, and intoned 'Sing and weep tears of joy, for on this day France has been made anew'; while at Notre Dame, a half sacred, half profane cantata, *Prise de la Bastille*, was performed, set to passages from the patriotic Book of Judith (Schama 1989: 502–12).

As the Revolution proceeded, popular fervour increased. A new flag, the tricolor, was adopted, along with a new national hymn, the 'Marseillaise', subsequently to become the national anthem. The King's title was changed from 'Louis, by the grace of God, King of France and Navarre' to 'Louis, by the grace of God and the constitutional law of the state, King of the French'. Regionalism was curbed, politically and culturally, to create *'la république, une et indivisible'*. From 1793, the French language was promoted throughout the land by the efforts of the Abbé Gregoire and of Barère, a member of the Jacobin Committee of Public Safety under Robespierre. The first plebiscites were held in two Papal enclaves, Avignon and Venaissin, to ascertain the (French) will of their populations. A national conscript army of citizens was mobilized, which defeated the invading armies of the monarchs at Valmy in September 1792 and thereafter; and in the flush of victory the 'patriots', as the revolutionaries called themselves, began to export to the 'liberated' territories they had conquered the revolutionary ideals of liberty, equality and fraternity. To celebrate this national renewal, great popular fêtes were organized in 1793 and 1794. Designed by David, to music by Gossec and poetry by André Chenier, they featured great processions and parades, hymns, colossal statues of Liberty and Nature, and rituals such as rebaptizing the soil with water, the release of thousands of doves of peace into the sky, and the descent of Robespierre, like some latterday Moses, from a giant plaster-and-cardboard mountain topped by a column with a statue of Hercules and a Tree of Liberty (Schama 1989: 746–50, 831–6).[1]

Modernism

What exactly was it that the French bourgeoisie was celebrating? Not just their accession to power and the end of aristocratic and clerical privilege. It was nothing less than the birth of a new nation of France, in the shape of the French Republic. In the work of the National Assembly and its successors, the process of building a new nation through constitutional change was pushed forward with immense vigour and zeal, in accordance with the rationalist blueprints of the *philosophes* of the Enlightenment.[2]

Such planned 'nation-building' was essentially a modern process, which found no real parallel before 1789. There had, it is true, been welfare programmes of enlightened monarchs in previous epochs, great construction projects, and even the large-scale 'modernization' of administration, from the laws of Hammurabi in ancient Babylon and the reforms of Augustus in Rome right up to the modernization programmes of Peter the Great in Russia and Joseph II of Austria. But there was no collective design to their work; it was conducted in the name of, and on behalf of, an individual or a ruling class. Nor was there any ideology of the sovereign people sharing a common history and culture, to whom supreme loyalty was owed and for whom great sacrifices must be made. There was no question in earlier epochs of mobilizing the people to participate in politics at the centre, nor of the need for men, let alone women, to become politically aware and active 'citizens'. Nor, as a result, was there any interest in providing an infrastructure and institutions which would cater to all the needs and interests of the citizens; nor, indeed, of instilling in the population at large, through mass, compulsory, standardized public education, the necessary attitudes and skills of a 'citizen', so as to maximize the power and well-being of the nation, and to imbue the citizenry with a purely secular respect for the laws of the nation.[3]

All this was new, a product of the centralizing programmes of the European absolutist monarchs from the sixteenth to the late eighteenth century, and of the growing reactions to their claims appearing first in the seventeenth-century Puritan revolts in Holland and England and reaching their culmination in the revolutions in the United States and France. It was, above all, in late eighteenth-century France that Pericles' exhortation to his fellow-Athenians in his Funeral Oration of 430BC, that they should 'fall in love with their city', became a living creed. Only then did his ideal of the active public-minded citizen of Athens strike a collective chord – no wonder that Rousseau and his followers looked back to classical Athens, Sparta and republican Rome for their models of civic solidarity and historic community. 'At this time, in fact', commented Durkheim on the French Revolution, 'under the influence of the general enthusiasm, things purely secular in nature became transformed into sacred things: these were the Fatherland, Liberty, Reason. A religion tended to become established which had its dogmas, symbols, altars and feasts' (Durkheim 1915: 214). As a process of 'nation-building' and as an ideology and movement, nationalism and its ideals of national autonomy, unity and identity, are relatively modern phenomena, which have placed at the centre of the political stage the sovereign, united and unique nation, and have made over the world in their image.[4]

The view that I have been outlining, and the historical developments that give it substance, may be called 'modernist'. Modernism comes in two forms, chronological and sociological. The first asserts, as I have been arguing, that national*ism* – the ideology, movement and symbolism – is relatively recent; the second, that nationalism is also qualitatively novel. In the second form, nationalism is an innovation, and not simply an updated version of something far older. Nothing like it existed before. But, this is not simply a matter of the perennial movement of history, it is a phenomenon brought into being by a wholly new epoch and an entirely novel set of conditions. Nationalism, in short, is a product of *modernity*, nothing less. It is this last assertion that marks out true modernism.

But it is not only nationalism that is modern. So are nations, national states, national identities and the whole 'inter-national' community. All these, for the modernist, are not just chronologically recent, they are also qualitatively novel. The French Revolution inaugurated not just a new ideology, but a new form of human community, a new kind of collective identity, a new type of polity and, in the end, a new kind of inter-state order. In the conjunction and inter-linking of these novel phenomena, is mirrored the new world order of modernity. But, equally, they reflect the new conditions characteristic of modernity.[5]

What are the specifically modern characteristics of national phenomena, and what are the main conditions that have encouraged the rise of nations, national states and nationalism? In their replies to these questions, the various kinds of modernism diverge, and I shall discuss some of the ensuing theories and debates in the next chapter. But, we may briefly distinguish the following varieties of the overall modernist paradigm:

1. Socioeconomic: nationalism and nations are derived, in this version, from such novel economic and social factors as industrial capitalism, regional inequality and class conflict. According to Tom Nairn and Michael Hechter, specifically national sentiments and ideals are aroused by relative deprivation between regions within modern states or classes across states, between the under-developed peripheral and the developed core regions or between core and peripheral elites backed by the newly mobilized 'masses' of the periphery (Hechter 1975; Nairn 1977).[6]
2. Sociocultural: nationalism and nations, according to Ernest Gellner, are sociologically necessary phenomena of the modern, industrial epoch, emerging in the transition of 'modernization'. Nations are expressions of a literate, school-transmitted 'high culture' supported by specialists and by a mass, standardized, compulsory, public education system. By training a mobile, literate workforce, nations in turn support industrialism, just as the latter encourages nationalism (Gellner 1964, ch. 7; 1973; and 1983).
3. Political: here, nations and nationalism are forged in and through the modern professionalized state, either directly

or in opposition to specific (imperial/colonial) states. For theorists like John Breuilly, Anthony Giddens and Michael Mann, not only is the modern state the best predictor of nations and nationalism, its relationship with society forms the crucible for a reintegrative nationalism, which is the inevitable concomitant of state sovereignty (Giddens 1985; Breuilly 1993; Mann 1995).

4. Ideological: the focus here is on the European origins and the modernity of nationalist ideology, its quasi-religious power and its role in breaking up empires and creating nations where none had existed. Elie Kedourie has traced nationalist ideologies to the impact of the Enlightenment and Kantian ideas of self-determination, and ultimately to medieval Christian millennial doctrines; and he has demonstrated their destructive effects on non-European peoples when a discontented intelligentsia adapted these chiliastic European doctrines to their native ethnic and religious traditions (Kedourie 1960; and 1971: Introduction).[7]

5. Constructionist: this is a rather different form of modernism in that, though it assumes that nations and nationalism are wholly modern, it emphasizes their socially constructed character. Nations, according to Eric Hobsbawm, owe much to 'invented traditions', which are products of social engineering and are created to serve the interests of ruling elites by channelling the energies of the newly enfranchised masses. Benedict Anderson, on the other hand, views the nation as an imagined political community which fills the void left by the decline of cosmic religions and monarchies at the point where new conceptions of time and 'print-capitalism' made it possible to imagine nations moving through linear time (Hobsbawm and Ranger 1983; Anderson 1991).

Despite their differences, these varieties of the paradigm of modernity all share a belief in what one might call 'structural modernism'. Theirs is no 'contingent modernism', no simple observation of an historical correlation between nationalism and modernity, but a belief in the inherently national, and nationalist, nature of modernity. It could not have been otherwise. In this view, modernity necessarily took the form of nations and just as inevitably produced nationalist ideologies and movements.

Perennialism

Today, modernism represents the dominant orthodoxy of scholarship in nationalism. For many, the modernity of nations, national states and nationalism is simply assumed; for others, it is something to be, more or less stridently, insisted upon. And yet it was not always so. Before the Second World War, many scholars subscribed to the view that, even if nationalist ideology was recent, nations had always existed in every period of history, and that many nations existed from time immemorial – a perspective that can be called 'perennialism'. It is probably fair to say that many members of the public hold a perennialist view to this day, especially where their own nations are concerned. But, in the nineteenth century and right up to the 1940s, many scholars subscribed to some version of perennialism, even those who, like Renan, favoured a more 'voluntarist' version of nationalism. This was partly aided by the popular equation of 'race' with 'nation', where the term 'race' often signified the separate culture of a descent group rather than hereditary and immutable biological traits and genes (and where today we might substitute the term 'ethnicity'). Perennialism was also encouraged by the idea of social evolution, with its emphasis upon gradualism, stages of progress and social and cultural cumulation. It was easy, even natural, to see nations as collective exemplars exhibiting these very qualities of gradualism, development and cumulation, especially for those who were attracted to the organic analogy. Nor should we overlook the great advances made in national historiography and archaeology, disciplines that, if they were fed by nationalist conceptions, also encouraged and bolstered those conceptions with apparently 'hard data' and the tangible remains of distant material cultures.[8]

Perennialism may also be encouraged by the idea that nations are 'natural' communities, and for some that was undoubtedly one of its attractions. But perennialism should not be confused with a naturalist conception of the nation, which is the basis of latterday 'primordialism'. Perennialists may subscribe to a 'primordial' conception of the nation, but equally they may not. All that is necessary for perennialism is a belief, founded on some empirical observation, that nations – or at least some nations – have existed for a long period of time, for whatever reason. They do not have to regard nations as natural, organic or primordial; indeed, they may, and often do, reject such ahistorical accounts. Perennialists need not be, and often are not, primordialists, and we need to keep the distinction in mind.

Perennialism comes in two main forms. The first, and more common variety, we may call 'continuous perennialism'. All that is asserted here is that particular nations have a long, continuous history, and can trace their origins back to the Middle Ages or, more rarely, antiquity. Here, the emphasis falls on *continuity*. While ruptures and discontinuities are not ignored, they are relativized by an emphasis on the slow rhythms of collective cultural identity. In fact, a nation's identity and history may not reach back beyond the Renaissance or the late medieval epoch, as, for example, with Sweden, Holland and Russia. Elsewhere, national origins may be traced still further back. Hugh Seton-Watson claimed that we could distinguish the 'old, continuous nations' from later examples that were deliberately created; the former included France, England, Scotland and Spain, and their longevity lent historical substance to the population's sense of immemorial nationhood. This is a position which, as we shall see, has recently received renewed support. But, in this case, no general model of perennialism is being proposed, only particular cases where historical records can be adduced which appear to demonstrate the longevity and continuity of specific nations. Nevertheless, insofar as this kind of perennialism can demonstrate the premodern origins of particular nations, it presents a serious challenge to the claims of modernism, and its belief that nations are the product of modernity (Seton-Watson 1977: ch. 2; see also Gillingham 1992; Hastings 1997).

The other main form we may term 'recurrent perennialism'. This makes a much bolder, general statement about the antiquity of nations. Particular nations, it says, are historical; they change with time. In Renan's words: 'They had their beginings, and they will end.' But the 'nation-in-general', as a category of human association, is perennial and ubiquitous, because it reappears in every period of history and is found in every continent of the globe. Here we are confronted by *recurrence* of the same type of collective cultural identity, even though it may be expressed in varied ways in different periods of history. Though particular nations may come and go, the idea of nationhood itself is a universal, disembedded phenomenon, and as such could apply to many cultural or political communities in every age and clime.[9]

Primordialism

Perennialism is a paradigm peculiar to (some) historians. 'Primordialism', in contrast, tends to be the preserve of social scientists – and organic nationalists. Its origins can be traced to Rousseau himself, with his call to flee urban corruption and return to 'nature' to recover a lost innocence. This 'naturalistic' spirit soon entered into the very definition of nationhood. We can see it at work already in the passage of the Abbé Siéyès which I quoted at the outset of this chapter. Nations, he asserts, must be conceived as individuals outside the social bond, in the 'state of nature'; they exist only 'in the natural order'. Indeed, they share with God the attributes of existing before all things and of originating everything. In other words, nations are 'primordial'; they exist in the first order of time, and lie at the root of subsequent processes and developments. Siéyès (and other followers of Rousseau) may not have used this language, let alone regarded himself as a 'primordialist'; but his are vast claims, and already in 1789 they are being used to justify the absolute sovereignty of the will of the nation, well before Fichte and other Romantics made similar claims for the German nation. This kind of 'naturalizing' discourse paved the way for the essentialist and organic forms of nationalism that I touched on earlier, but it also influenced the more voluntarist kinds of nationalism.[10]

Biology and culture

This, then, is one variety of primordialism, that of an organicist nationalism. More recently, we have witnessed the rise of two other kinds of primordialism. The first is a *sociobiological* version, which holds that nations, ethnic groups and races can be traced to the underlying genetic reproductive drives of individuals and their use of strategies of 'nepotism' and 'inclusive fitness' to maximize their gene pools. For Pierre van den Berghe, these strategies are used to extend the individual's gene pool beyond immediate kinship ties, to wider ethnic kin. In this case, the cultural group is treated as a wider kin network, and cultural symbols (language, religion, colour, etc.) are used as markers of biological affinity. For Van den Berghe, this is an eminently rational strategy, since for the most part *myths* of ethnic origins correspond to *real* biological origins. That is why people who are not directly related are prepared to treat unknown co-ethnics as 'kin' and to nurture and defend them as if they were (Van den Berghe 1978 and 1995).

There are a number of difficulties with this account. The most obvious is the problem of generalizing from the level of individual reproductive behaviour to that of collective, and political, action. Even the extended family is too small to be politically significant, except in a few cases, and it is difficult to see how large-scale sociopolitical developments can be explained by recourse to individual or kin behaviour. A second, related difficulty is that myths of origin are rarely correlated with actual biological origins, assuming that these can be traced. As Walker Connor demonstrated (1994: 202), myths of origin generally fail to correspond to what we know about actual descent lines. Typically, nations will have several ethnic strains and origins, whereas myths of origin and descent presuppose a single, agreed or official source. Finally, by introducing the level of 'cultural signs', Van den Berghe dilutes the rigour and purity of his reductionist biological account, and suggests a much greater role for cultural and social factors that would necessarily diminish the influence of genetic factors.

A second, and more influential, version of primordialism holds that ethnic groups and nations are formed on the basis of attachments to the 'cultural givens' of social existence. Both Edward Shils and Clifford Geertz showed how 'primordial' ties persisted alongside the secular, civil ties, even in industrial societies. Geertz, in particular, contrasted primordial attachments with the civil ties of the rational order of modern polities and society. In the new states of Africa and Asia, Geertz discerned two powerful drives: for personal identity, based on the continuing strength and hold of attachments to kin, race, language, religion, customs and territory; and for efficiency and stability, which finds its expression in the civil ties of the new political order. In fact, the desire for order and efficiency simply exacerbates primordial attachments among ethnic groups in the new states, because sovereign state power and its patronage becomes a new prize over which to fight and a new challenge with which to contend (Shils 1957; Geertz 1973).

Today, 'primordialism' has acquired pejorative connotations of fixity, essentialism and naturalism. This image is based partly on the unjustified association of primordialism with an organic type of nationalism, partly on a misreading of Geertz's celebrated essay, 'The integrative revolution'. In claiming that ethnic attachments and nations spring from the 'cultural givens' of social existence, and that many peoples' 'sense of self is bound up in the gross actualities of blood, race, language, locality, religion or tradition', Geertz is not embracing an organic naturalism. For he immediately introduces a vital qualification, when he says:

> By a primordial attachment is meant one that stems from the 'givens' – or more precisely, as culture is inevitably involved in such matters, the assumed 'givens' of social existence . . . These congruities of blood, speech, custom and so on, are seen to have an ineffable, and at times, overpowering coerciveness in and of themselves. (Geertz 1973: 259–60)

In this passage, the words 'assumed' and 'are seen to', and the reference to culture, tell us that for Geertz primordial attachments rest on perceptions and beliefs, and that it is not the intrinsic nature of these attachments that makes them 'given' and powerful; rather, it is human beings who see these ties as givens, and attribute to them an overpowering coerciveness. What Geertz is claiming, and what is so important about the primordialist contribution, is that we, as individuals and members of collectivities, *feel and believe in* the primordiality of our *ethnies* and nations – their naturalness, longevity and power – and that if we ignore these beliefs and feelings, we evade one of the central problems of explanation in the field of ethnicity and nationalism.

For a key question that confronts any theory of nations and nationalism is why they generate so much passion and such strong attachments. In seeking to answer this question, primordialists point to the durability and apparent coerciveness of these attachments, and to the need to take into account what we may call a 'participants' primordialism', that is, the participants' vivid sense of the primordial nature of their own collective cultural identities. But this, in itself, is no answer, as Eller and Coughlan have pointed out. We need to know why so many people share this sense of primordiality and feel these attachments. This requires a rational, empirical analysis of ethnic attachments, not an assertion of the a priori nature and emotional content of such ties. In reply, Steven Grosby has made the interesting suggestion that people base their feelings of attachment on certain beliefs about the life-enhancing nature of such collectivities, and the life-sustaining properties of kinship and, more especially, of territory. This is a thought-provoking proposition, but it can only point us in a certain direction. In itself, it can hardly serve as an historical or sociological explanation for the various kinds of cultural community, or for their transformations over time. Nor can such a paradigm shed light on why people become attached to certain historic collectivities and not others (for example, Germany rather than Prussia), and why such attachments vary in scope, intensity and timing.[11]

The instrumentalist critique

This is where an 'instrumentalist' approach can help. Like primordialism, the instrumentalist approach was pioneered in respect of ethnicity rather than nations or nationalism. It came to prominence in the 1960s and 1970s in the United

States, in the debate about (white) ethnic persistence in what was supposed to have been an effective melting-pot. While Will Herberg had spoken of a triple American melting-pot (Protestant, Catholic, Jew), Nathan Glazer and Daniel Moynihan showed how the various ethnic groups of New York adapted to an American lifestyle while retaining their identities. This sparked a lively debate through the 1970s on the degree to which ethnic groups in the United States should be seen as interest or pressure groups behaving instrumentally in the political marketplace – groups that had in later generations increasingly shed their cultural distinctiveness or were treating it as largely symbolic and optional. The implication was that ethnic leaders and elites used their cultural groups as sites of mass mobilization and as constituencies in their competition for power and resources, because they found them more effective than social classes.[12]

It was not long before an instrumentalist approach was applied to the genesis of nations. A particularly clear example can be found in the seminal debate between Paul Brass and Francis Robinson on the origins of Pakistan. For Brass, Pakistan was created by Muslim elites who manipulated Islamic symbolic resources in order to mobilize the Muslim masses of northwest India, at a time when British policies appeared to turn against Muslim interests. For Robinson, it was the other way round: existing Muslim attachments and ideologies (notably of the *umma*) persuaded the Muslim elites of the need to safeguard the Muslim community and culture by seeking greater autonomy for the Muslims of the North-west United Provinces and Bengal. Yet, the distance between these two readings of the situation is not as great as it seems. Brass, for example, conceded the importance of existing traditions, especially where there was a rich cultural heritage and an institutional (for example, religious) framework, while Robinson was careful to insist on the political rationality of Muslim elite actions (Brass 1979 and 1991; Robinson 1979).

Nevertheless, in other hands, the instrumentalist approach can be used to uphold a strictly modernist paradigm. This is the case with John Breuilly's political theory of nationalism, which I consider in more detail in the next chapter. For the moment, I want to concentrate on his methodological aims. These he sets out in a concluding chapter of the revised 1993 version of his book, *Nationalism and the State*. Though his definition of nationalism refers to culture, Breuilly rejects any idea of cultural *identity* as a defining characteristic of nationalism (which he treats as a strictly political and modern phenomenon), because he thinks that would lead us back to an irrational primordialist 'need to belong'. Yet he also admits that nationalism 'derives much of its power from the half-truths it embodies', adding:

> People do yearn for communal membership, do have a strong sense of us and them, of territories as homelands, of belonging to culturally defined and bounded worlds which give their lives meaning. Ultimately, much of this is beyond rational analysis and, I believe, the explanatory powers of the historian. (Breuilly 1993: 401)

Perhaps so. But the effect, in Breuilly's hands, is to limit the range of meaning of the concept of nationalism to a purely political – and strictly instrumental – usage. Nationalism becomes simply an argument through which sub-elites can mobilize people, coordinate the diverse interests of social groups and legitimate their actions, in order to seize or retain power in the modern state. It is a purely political argument, which says that there exists a nation with an explicit and peculiar character, that its interests and values take priority over all others and that the nation must be as independent as possible. For Breuilly, nationalism is not about identity, unity, authenticity, dignity, the homeland or anything else, save political power, that is, political goals in the modern state. Nationalism is simply an instrument for achieving political goals, and as such it can only emerge under modern conditions. Anything else is beyond the pale of rational analysis (ibid.: 2).

Rationality, modernity, politics: this trinity is a recurrent feature of instrumentalism, and represents a closure of argument. Its effect is to delegitimize alternative approaches and to disqualify every paradigm of nationalism except the modernist. But, in practice, such a self-denying ordinance only serves to vacate ground which should come under the scrutiny not only of rational analysis, but of an analysis that would admit far more to its scrutiny than the top-down, elite-driven and rational choice political models currently on offer among so many modernists.

Ethno-symbolism

One such alternative is the kind of socio-historical and cultural analysis encouraged by an 'ethno-symbolic' paradigm. This is the last of the four main paradigms in the field – a possible fifth, the 'postmodernist', which I shall consider in the last chapter, remains too fragmentary and sketchy as yet to merit the designation of 'paradigm'. In contrast to the modernist, perennialist and primordialist paradigms of ethnicity and nationalism, historical ethno-symbolism focuses particularly on the subjective elements in the persistence of *ethnies*, the formation of nations and the impact of nationalism. This does not mean that it takes 'objective' factors for granted or excludes them from the purview of its analysis; only that it gives more weight to subjective elements of memory, value, sentiment, myth and symbol, and that it thereby seeks to enter and understand the 'inner worlds' of ethnicity and nationalism.

Ethno-symbolic perspectives share a number of concerns. The first is to move away from the exclusively elite-oriented kinds of analysis characteristic of modernism. In contrast, ethno-symbolists stress the relationship between various elites and the lower strata ('the people') they aim to represent. But this is not a one-way relationship. The non-elites, partly through their cultural traditions and partly in consequence of their vernacular mobilization, influence the intelligentsia, political leaders and bourgeoisie, by constraining their innovations within certain cultural parameters and by providing motifs and personnel for their cultural projects and political goals. A good example of this was the intellectual and popular movement of the Gaelic revival in late nineteenth-century Ireland, richly documented by John Hutchinson (1987: chs 4–5); here, the traditions of the peasantry and Catholic lower classes provided parameters and cultural materials for the revivalist formulations of the Irish intellectuals.

A second common concern is with long-term analysis – that is, with the analysis of social and cultural patterns over *la longue durée*. Only by conducting investigations over several generations and even centuries can scholars reveal the complex relationships between past, present and future and the place of *ethnies* and nations in history. This enables us to avoid the anachronism of a 'retrospective nationalism', which would read into the conditions and politics of earlier epochs the collective goals and nationalist aspirations of the present, while at the same time doing justice to the many, varied forms of collective cultural identities characteristic of earlier ages. Above all, an ethno-symbolic approach directs attention to the ways in which earlier forms of collective identity may influence the rise of nations, while allowing for the many ruptures and discontinuities of the historical record.[13]

Third, this means that analysis of the rise of nations and nationalism is placed within a framework of earlier collective cultural identities, and especially of ethnic communities or *ethnies*. However, the relationship of nations to *ethnies* is a complex one; there is no simple linear progression. From one angle, nations can be regarded as specialized (territorialized, politicized, mass-public, etc.) forms of *ethnie*; from another angle, nations and *ethnies* are both forms of collective cultural identity that may coexist or compete with each other, with several *ethnies* often residing within the boundaries of the political community of the nation. Nationalism and nations, for this paradigm, far from being tied exclusively to modernity, are part of a wider ethno-cultural 'family' of collective identities and aspirations, as my earlier discussion of definitions of the concept of the nation (in chapter l) suggested. This may also explain why nationalists so often seek to rediscover and appeal to cultural and symbolic repertoires within the antecedent populations with whom they claim a deep cultural continuity.[14]

Another important shared concern is the problem of collective passion and attachment. Where modernists usually fail to address this problem, or only touch on it in general terms, and where perennialists simply fail to treat it as a problem, because they assume the continuity or recurrence of nations everywhere, ethno-symbolists regard it as a key problem for understanding ethnicity and nationalism. Unlike the primordialists who had at most a metaphysical answer, ethno-symbolists propose historical and/or sociological explanations which address the reasons for the continuing emotional attachments of so many people to their ethnic communities and nations, and for their capacity for fanatical terrorism and self-sacrifice on their behalf.

Finally, because of their concern with the popular, moral and emotional dimensions of ethnic and national identities, ethno-symbolist approaches can help us to grasp both the persistence and the transformations of these collective cultural identities. By relating national identities to prior ethnic ties, and showing the influence of subjective dimensions of shared symbols, myths and memories, ethno-symbolism throws light on the continuing hold exercised by modern nations over so many people today. For the same reasons, an ethno-symbolic paradigm can inspire alternative explanations of the intensity and contents of current ethnic conflicts to the usual economic and political accounts. These alternative accounts give due weight to the key symbolic issues that so often prove the most intractable – as witnessed in the Muslim–Hindu clashes over the mosque at Ayodhya, the Orange Order marches in Ulster, or the status of Jerusalem. For, as the name suggests, 'ethno-symbolism' shifts the focus of analysis away from purely external political and economic, or sociobiological, factors to the cultural ones of symbol, memory, myth, value and tradition.[15]

As with the other paradigms, ethno-symbolism takes various forms. John Armstrong leans more to a perennialist standpoint, which tends to downplay the distinction between nations and ethnic identities (though he does make a distinction between nations before and after 1800, i.e. the watershed of 'nationalism'). This is partly because Armstrong adopts a phenomenological account, which sees ethnic identities as shifting clusters of perceptions, sentiments and attitudes. At the same time, he employs the cultural and symbolic boundary analysis pioneered by Fredrik Barth, and stresses the need for investigations of 'myth-symbol complexes' over *la longue durée* to understand the persistence of ethnicity (Armstrong 1982 and 1995; cf. Barth 1969: Introduction).

John Hutchinson, on the other hand, has adopted a more Weberian approach to distinguish modern cultural from political types of nationalism, and uncover the dynamics of the cultural forms. Hutchinson is also concerned with the part played by the past in both premodern ethnic revivals and modern nationalisms, and the way in which premodern cultural repertoires of myths, memories and symbols can be 'carried' by institutions into the modern epoch. My own analysis is concerned with a third problem: the nature and role of nations in history. While acknowledging the modernity of nationalism, the ideology, movement and symbolism, and the recent formation of most nations, I have become interested in the possibility of nations prior to nationalism, at least in a few cases, and its implications. But, in general, my approach has focused on the way that prior, and often premodern, ethnic ties and *ethnies* have influenced, and in some cases formed the basis for, subsequent nations and nationalisms (Hutchinson 1987 and 1994; A. D. Smith 1986 and 1991).

Conclusion

Ethno-symbolism arose out of a dissatisfaction with the claims of the rival modernist and perennialist paradigms, and the explanatory failure of primordialism. If, on the one hand, nations are neither continuously immemorial nor recurrent, and if, on the other hand, nations are neither all recent and novel, nor just products of modernization, then it becomes necessary to search for another paradigm that would encompass and do justice to the oft-remarked duality, or Janus-nature, of nations and nationalism. Such a paradigm, while not neglecting external political, geopolitical and economic factors, would focus on subjective symbolic and socio-cultural elements, encourage more nuanced perspectives and approaches, and thereby address the vital symbolic issues of ethnic identity, myth and memory that so often prove intractable. Neither perennialism nor modernism sought to enter the inner world of nationalism; and without such a focus, ethno-symbolists argue, there is little chance of understanding other peoples' nationalisms and, as a result, of beginning to address the grievances and sentiments that fuel their conflicts.

The debates between adherents of the four paradigms have taken place on two levels: theory and history. Put baldly, of the four paradigms, the modernists have been strong on theory, but rather weak on history, whereas perennialists have been rather stronger on history, but weak on theory. Primordialism has either a flawed theory or none, and little or no history, being reductionist (sociobiology) or largely speculative or ahistorical (cultural primordialism). As for the ethnosymbolists, they have evolved no theory, only approaches. But, as one might expect, they are concerned with macrohistory and its sociocultural elements, and, as such, they provide, in my view, a necessary corrective to the often sweeping claims of adherents of the other main paradigms.

4
Theories

In this chapter I want to consider some of the explanations of nationalism put forward by adherents of the four paradigms, and the problems and debates they have generated. In a field as vast as this, no attempt can be made to be comprehensive. But I hope this selection will give some idea of the main issues and lines of argument in the field. Rather than listing all the main explanations *seriatim*, I have chosen to present them in the form of imagined 'debates'. In this way, I hope to demonstrate the innovative and lively nature of recent scholarship on nationalism since the 1960s, and reveal more vividly the contours of rival positions in the field.

Ideology and Industrialism

If we leave aside the claims of sociobiology, there was until very recently really only one theory in the field.[1] The theory in question was put forward in 1964 by Ernest Gellner in the seventh chapter of his *Thought and Change*. The context of his theory was both empirical observation of the rising tide of nationalism in Morocco, where Gellner did his anthropological fieldwork, and the intellectualist challenge of his colleague Elie Kedourie at the London School of Economics.

Kedourie had argued that nationalism 'was a doctrine invented in Europe at the beginning of the nineteenth century' (1960: 1), more specifically in Germany in 1806–7 by Johann Gottlob Fichte in his seminal *Addresses to the German Nation*. Its causes were both intellectual and social. On the one hand, nationalism was a doctrine of the will preached by German Romantics, and represented a collectivization of Immanuel Kant's ideal of the autonomy of the will and its application to cultural and, especially, linguistic groups, which were the focus of Johann Gottfried Herder's concern for cultural diversity. For Kedourie, both Kant's emphasis on the good will as the free will and Herder's commitment to the authentic experience of indigenous culture groups were products of the Enlightenment rationalist quest for moral and intellectual certainty.[2]

On the other hand, nationalism was a subversive and revolutionary answer to the malaise and alienation of German, and European, intellectuals at odds with tradition and with their fathers, and excluded by bureaucratic absolutism from the power that they felt was their due as a result of their enlightened education. For Kedourie (1960), nationalism was a movement of alienated youth, a 'children's crusade'. A doctrine born under such auspices could only bode ill; and so it proved to be. For the millennial nationalism of the disoriented intellectuals has brought nothing but terror and destruction in its wake, especially in ethnically mixed areas.

Gellner took issue with a number of Kedourie's assertions. To begin with, he exculpated Kant as the chief architect of nationalism; Kant's autonomy of the good will applied only to individuals, not to groups. Second, he saw nationalism in a rather more positive light, not, to be sure, in terms of its own valuation of itself, which Gellner dismissed, but as an ideological instrument for social development. Third, while the critical intellectuals were the undoubted leaders of the movement, they required the support of the lower classes, the 'proletariat', by which Gellner meant the uprooted peasantry flocking to the city and its shanty towns. Finally, though he agreed with Kedourie that nationalism was modern, Gellner thought this was no accident or 'invention'. Rather, it was an inevitable consequence of the transition to modernity in which all societies of the world had been involved since the eighteenth century. It followed that, though nationalism was logically contingent, it was sociologically necessary – in the modern world (Gellner 1964: ch. 7).

Gellner then went on to outline his theory of why this was so. Modernization, by which Gellner meant industrialization and its social and cultural concomitants, was transforming all societies just as the neolithic revolution had done some 8,000 years earlier. It was producing a new type of industrial society, requiring a mobile, literate and numerate workforce, able to engage in semantic work and context-free commu-nication. Whereas in earlier, agrarian societies, literacy was confined to the few and human beings were bound together by the structure of roles and institutions, often based on kinship, in modern, industrial societies, 'culture replaced structure'. That is, 'language and culture' became the new cement for an atomized society, one based on uprooted, detraditionalized individuals who had to be integrated into the industrial machine and whose new and only acceptable identity was citizenship based upon literacy and culture. Modernization, therefore, eroded tradition and traditional societies, and threw up language and culture as the sole basis for identity. Today, said Gellner, 'we are all clerks', and to be clerks and citizens, we must be taught in the new mass, com-pulsory, standardized, public education systems provided by the state (ibid.).

But there was another, darker effect of the great tide of modernization. As it swept outwards from its West European heartlands, it divided areas by the uneven, jagged quality of its movement, hitting successive regions at different times, rates and intensities. It also divided populations: into the old-time residents of the great urban centres, and the new, uprooted proletarians who were increasingly excluded from vital urban resources such as housing, employment and education. Now, if the excluded shared their language and culture with the old-time residents, the ensuing discontent was likely to turn to class conflict. But, if they did not, if the newcomers had a different colour, language or religion from the old urban residents, then to class conflict would be added ethnic antagonism. In these circumstances, the proletarian newcomers would be tempted to listen to the calls of their co-cultural intelligentsia to join them in hiving off and setting up a wholly new nation; at this point, two nationalisms gave rise to two nations either side of the divide. So, beneath its florid rhetoric, nationalism turned out to be an objectively necessary, practical programme (ibid.: ch. 7; see also Gellner 1973)

Later, Gellner reformulated his theory in a number of ways. First, he demonstrated why there could be neither nations nor nationalisms in premodern epochs. There was simply no need or use for either in 'agro-literate' societies, ruled as they were by tiny elites who did not share their culture with the great mass of food-producers beneath them, and who saw no reason to do so. The latter, in turn, were subdivided into a host of overlapping linguistic cultures, and as a result their grievances could never take national form. Even the clergy, the only stratum with the desire to monopolize culture, had insufficient resources to do so (Gellner 1983).

Second, Gellner explained in more detail the type of culture characteristic of industrial societies. Here, he used the term 'high culture' to mean not an elite culture, but a literate and standardized public 'garden' culture, supported by specialists and a system of 'exo-socialization' or public education. This he contrasted with the many wild, uncultivated 'low' cultures, which were characteristic of premodern societies, but which could not survive in modern conditions – either they had to be turned into high cultures, or they would perish. Third, Gellner sharpened his differences with perennialists and primordialists, not only by mocking the claims of nationalist ideologues, but by emphasizing the sociological and historical novelty of nations and nationalism, which, though it might use elements from existing (premodern) cultures, actually did not need them: 'The cultural shreds and patches used by nationalism are often arbitrary historical inventions. Any old shred and patch would have served as well' (ibid.: 56). The same point was put even more forcefully in his last public lecture on the subject, when he argued that nations were created in the eighteenth century and nothing before then really mattered. Nations, like Adam, did not need to have navels (Gellner 1996).

All this gave the later version of Gellner's theory (1983) a much more materialist, and determinist, outlook. Nations and nationalism were now seen as necessary and functional for industrial modernity, just as the latter became necessarily nationalist. A particular kind of socioeconomic formation required a certain kind of culture and ideology, and vice-versa (see also Gellner 1997).[3]

This was also the position taken by Tom Nairn in *The Break-up of Britain* (1977). There, he argued that the unevenness of development was the prime mover of nationalism. Only, for Nairn, it was an uneven wave of capitalism rather than industrialism. Moreover, capitalism did not come to the periphery alone; it came in the 'fetters' of imperialism. Metropolitan capitalist bourgeoisies were greatly aided in the exploitation of the colonies by the administrators and armies of the great Western powers. Faced with this onslaught, the elites of the colonized periphery were helpless. They had no guns, no wealth, no technology and no skills to match those of the imperialists. But they did have one asset. In the helplessness of their condition – the true meaning of 'underdevelopment' – they appealed to the one thing that they had in plentiful supply: people. People was all they had, but it proved a potent weapon. They mobilized 'the people' and invited them into history, writing the invitation card in their language and culture, and channelling their 'mass sentiments' into national resistance movements. That is why nationalism is always a populist, romantic and cross-class movement, and why it feeds off the ethnic sentiments of the masses (Nairn 1977: chs 2, 9).[4]

Does this then mean that the character and ideals of nationalism are always functions of its social location and geopolitical situation? Are the elites as devoid of real agency and choice as the masses, and are their ideas irrelevant in a situation ultimately determined by global socioeconomic processes? That is undoubtedly the implication of modernization theory; as Gellner himself put it: 'The philopher-kings of the "underdeveloped world" all act as westernisers, and all talk like *narodniks*' (Gellner 1964: 171).

To the ideological determinism of a Kedourie, modernization theory counterposes a socioeconomic determinism. For Gellner, in particular, ideology – nationalist ideology – is largely irrelevant, and erroneous. Nations were not predestined, nor do human beings naturally require a nationality. It is modernity that requires nations and makes nationalities seem natural. It is modernity that inevitably comes in the shape of 'nationalism', and it is nationalism that creates nations: 'Nationalism . . . invents nations where they do not exist, but it does need some pre-existing differentiating marks to work on, even if . . . these are purely negative' (ibid.: 168). I shall return later to the question of differentiating marks. For the moment I want to concentrate on the way in which ideas, and specifically 'ideologies' (of nationalism), are removed from the causal chain. The difficulty here is not simply one of determinism, the lack of elite choices, but of 'foreshortening', by which key elements and important stages of a meaningful and causally adequate explanation are omitted.[5]

Gellner argues that nations are created by 'nationalism', which in turn is the cultural form assumed by modernity, that is, modern industrialism. Nationalism in this theory becomes a necessary cultural form, a 'high culture'. It has no active or directive power, and makes no separate causal contribution; it simply mediates industrialism through the prism of culture. This suggests that it does not really matter which form or what intensity 'nationalism' has, nor which nations it (that is, industrialism) conjures into being, and when or where. All this is secondary to the global necessity of 'nationalism-in-general', and cannot be illuminated by an explanation of that necessity. So, the theory cannot tell us why nationalism is more benign in some nations and states, more virulent in others, why it creates some nations and destroys others, why we encounter here religious nationalisms, there revolutionary ones, and there again racist or fascist nationalisms.[6]

Gellner's 'nationalism', in other words, has little or no connection with what most people mean by the term: the ideologies and movements under whose banner people have sought unity, identity and autonomy for their nation. Admittedly, Kedourie in his turn had placed too much weight on the role of these ideas and movements, though he sought to correct this imbalance in his later introduction to an anthology of nationalist writings in Africa and Asia (Kedourie 1971). But, we may ask, did he not have a point when he showed how the messianic promise of nationalist ideology was eagerly embraced by the disoriented and alienated young 'marginal men', caught between the traditions of their communities and the illusory promises of the West?[7]

For Kedourie, nationalism is a doctrine of the will. For Gellner, it is the cultural form taken by industrialism. For Kedourie, nationalist ideals are powerful in their own right; indeed, they have the power to lead people astray, to disorient them and ultimately to destroy them. For Gellner, ideas have no such power, and the ideology of nationalism merely masks the true workings of industrial culture. But, if that is the case, one would have expected more uniformity, more regularity, in a world of nations, particularly in the character of nations and the contents of their ideologies – and in their consequences. That this is so clearly *not* the case points to a glaring omission in modernization theory: it has no place for the role of individuals and their ideals. In this respect, Kedourie's account, for all its flaws, provides a valuable corrective. It tells us more – and with great insight – about the inner workings of nationalist ideologies and intellectuals; and, while its diffusionist thesis about the spread of nationalism is quite inadequate, it reveals much about both the philosophical background of nationalism in Europe and the motivations and situations of a class of educated young men in Africa and Asia. Kedourie's account, for all its ideological determinism, reminds us of the truth in Durkheim's dictum that ideas, once born, have a life of their own.

Reason and Emotion

The debate between Kedourie and Gellner was one that took place within the modernist camp, and it was a genuine debate. The remaining arguments spring from the different positions taken by scholars working within rival paradigms, and my reconstruction of their arguments takes the form of imagined debates.

Such a difference of position and debate concerns the question of motivation, and specifically why people should feel, and become, nationalists. For Michael Hechter, this is largely a question of 'rational choice'. Moving away from his earlier purely structural account of 'internal colonialism' in the developed West, Hechter (1988) embraced a general theory of solidarity which owed much to rational choice analysis and its methodological individualism. Of course, the 'sovereign preferences of individuals' operate within a structure that determines, more or less, the constraints under which they act; but the course of action individuals adopt is, within these limits, chosen rationally, that is, in accordance with a calculation of costs and benefits. Ethnic groups are salient examples of solidary groups able to confer private rewards and punishments and to control information, as well as sanction criminals and free-riders.[8]

Can such a general schema illuminate questions such as national secession and nationalist violence? Secession is usually a risky course of action, and only private inducements, such as the prospect of jobs, can persuade the middle classes to join such a cause; and even then the likelihood of secession will depend on perceptions of the strength of the host state (Hechter 1992: 273–5).

As for nationalist violence, this is usually a function of state repression of oppositional groups, and is therefore carefully calibrated: 'There is ample evidence that nationalist groups employ violence strategically as a means to produce their joint goods, among which sovereignty looms large' (Hechter 1995: 62). For Hechter, the case of Northern Ireland shows that nationalist violence is limited, because a weak solidaristic nationalist group is confronted by a strong state apparatus able to repress secession. Violence will escalate only where a weakened state faces a highly solidaristic nationalism.[9]

This is the context of Hechter's most recent and sustained exposition of the problem. Here he argues that nationalism, the principle that the nation should be congruent with the unit of governance (not necessarily the state), is modern because it is a function of a global modernizing move towards direct rule. In premodern imperial polities, peripheral elites were generally left to rule over their regional populations under the loose authority of the empire, in a system of indirect rule, which by and large satisfied all parties. But, in the modern world, centralizing states become the norm, and regional (peripheral) populations come to be ruled by strangers unaware of their needs. So, only then does it begin to make sense for peripheral elites to embrace a nationalist policy of seeking independence; and that is why we only find nationalism in the modern world (Hechter 2000, esp. chs 2–3).

Here, Hechter directly addresses the criticism that his previous 'rational choice' accounts had little or nothing to say about the specificity of nationalism; the schema could apply to any kind of revolt or violence. Now, because of the change in types of authority, it makes sense to appeal specifically to 'nationalism' as a means of binding the peripheral population to the peripheral elite against the centralizing state through a common 'nation'. But, we may ask, why should the population follow their lead? Hechter's various accounts presume an underlying *individual* rationality in nationalism, which leaves no place for collective values, memories, symbols and emotions, only for the fungible goods of wealth, status and power. But are these really enough to explain the passion and wide appeal of nationalism? Can we ignore, for example, the effect of memories of previous wars and atrocities in moments of political crisis, irrespective of the benefits that might accrue to individuals if they joined particular nationalist revolts or movements?[10]

For Walker Connor and Joshua Fishman, this would be out of the question. Nationalism can never be simply a rational quest for collective goods, for it is, above all, love of an ethno-nation – as opposed to patriotism, which is loyalty to the territorial state. The 'civic nationalism', which modernists prefer and which is really only patriotism, is indeed a 'rational' kind of loyalty and can be rationally explained, argues Connor; but 'ethno-nationalism', which is the only nationalism, can never be rationally explained. It can only be analysed – and invoked. And that is exactly what nationalist leaders have done, and they have been far more successful than the scholars, because they intuitively understood that 'at the core of ethnopsychology is the sense of shared blood, and they have not hesitated to appeal to it' (Connor 1994: 197). For Walker Connor, the nation is 'a group of people who *believe* they are ancestrally related. It is the largest grouping that shares such a belief' (ibid.: 212; italics in original). The nation is ultimately based on felt kinship ties; its essence is a psychological bond that joins a people and differentiates it from everyone else, in the subconscious conviction of its members (ibid.: 92).

Of course, the conviction of common kinship ties, and the myth of shared ethnic descent, need not, and usually does not, accord with real biological descent and what we know of factual history. But then, what is important in the study of nationalism is not what is, but what is *felt* to be, the case. The conviction of common ancestry is based not on facts and reason, but on a powerful and *non*-rational (not *ir*rational) feeling of the members. Its appeal and stimuli can be studied, but it cannot be rationally explained. To try to do so is to miss the depth and power of national conviction.[11]

This is an original and powerful perspective, and it sounds like a case of extreme perennialism, if not primordialism – a view reinforced by Connor's analysis of the relationship between ethnic groups and nations. For Connor, nations are really only self-aware ethnic groups. Whereas ethnic groups may be discerned and defined by outsiders, and need not be self-aware, nations must be self-defined. Ethnic groups can therefore be seen as 'pre-national peoples' and potential nations. Nations, on the other hand, are fully self-aware communities, and since they are mass phenomena, it follows that they can only come into being when the majority of their members are nationally aware. In practice, and in democracies, this means that the majority must participate in the life of the nation; and for Connor that in turn means that they must be enfranchised (ibid.: 98–103).

Connor's perspective, it transpires, ends up being the very opposite of perennialism, let alone primordialism. It turns out to be a radical variety of modernism, albeit of a rather special kind. For Connor concludes that nations came into existence only at the beginning of the twentieth century, when the great majority of their members, including women, began to participate – and vote – in public life. Of course, before that time, we can never know what the peasant masses thought or felt. But it is really only after 1789, when the dogma that 'alien rule is illegitimate rule' began to infect ethnically aware peoples, that nations came into existence, by stages. And in this process, modernization and mass communications proved to be important catalysts. For, by bringing people into regular contact, modernization has paradoxically separated them and made them self-aware, where before, under imperial rule, they would have become culturally assimilated (ibid.: 169–174).

This is a strange conclusion in the context. It seems quite at odds with the spirit of Connor's work, and it begs several questions of definition and historical interpretation. It is as if a national modernism was riding on the back of an ethnic perennialism. But closer inspection suggests that we are faced with only a chronological, or 'contingent', modernism. Nations, for Connor, are not really that different, qualitatively, from ethnic groups, nor are they the product of modernization, as sociological, or 'structural', modernism insists. The basic reason for this is that, for Connor, nations, like ethnic groups, are phenomena of mass psychology and ultimately of felt kinship.

Is there, then, no rationality to nationalism? Is it, as the Romantics would have us believe, simply a matter of blood and emotion? Perhaps Joshua Fishman has a point, when he claims that ethnicity is a matter of 'being', as well as 'knowing' and 'doing', and that

> Ethnicity has always been experienced as a kinship phenomenon, a continuity within the self and within those who share an intergenerational link to common ancestors. Ethnicity is partly experienced as being 'bone of their bone, flesh of their flesh, and blood of their blood'. The human body itself is viewed as an expression of ethnicity and ethnicity is commonly felt to be in the blood, bones and flesh. (Fishman 1980: 84–5)

On the other hand, don't people – including nationalists – carefully calculate, as Hechter claims, the odds of nationalist revolts, the costs of joining nationalist movements and the benefits of '*fraternité*' (and, now, '*sororité*')? Even if we concede, as I think we must, that there are powerful subjective elements in nations and nationalism, that people sometimes 'think with their blood' and, in Connor's words, 'do not voluntarily die for things that are rational' (1994: 206), it does not follow that these phenomena are non-rational and cannot be explained in structural and cultural terms. Nor that, because we might *define* nations and nationalism in social psychological terms, we cannot, in principle, *explain* them in rational terms. It may be difficult, but the two are by no means incompatible. Because modernists such as Gellner and Hechter pay little attention to social psychological variables, that does not mean that we have to embrace a psychological (and hence 'non-rational'?) position in order to analyse nations and nationalism and forgo historical and sociological explanations. On the contrary: the nature of the subject-matter makes it all the more important that we do so, provided that our understanding of 'explanation' is such as to include the various cultural, social and social psychological elements of emotion, will, symbol, memory and felt kinship that Walker Connor rightly emphasizes and that the instrumentalists tend to ignore or disallow.[12]

Politics and Culture

The third issue that I want to consider revolves around the role of the modern state and, more generally, politics, in the formation of nations and the development of nationalism. We might call it the problem of cultural nationalism or, more broadly, cultural identity.

Since the early 1980s, a number of post-Marxist theories have stressed the relative autonomy of the state and adopted a more Weberian outlook on the primacy of politics. All the approaches and models in question are modernist and instrumentalist. This is as true of Michael Mann's, as it is of Anthony Giddens's interpretations of nationalism. For both, it is the modern state, centralized, professionalized and territorialized, that conjures nationalisms and engenders what Anthony Giddens calls the 'cultural sensibility of sovereignty, the concomitant of the coordination of administrative power within the bounded nation-state' (Giddens 1985: 219). Similarly, Michael Mann, speaking of the state-supporting nationalisms of Britain and France, is equally clear: 'But the clarity of focus on the nation as coterminous with the state cries out for a predominantly political explanation' (Mann 1995: 48). And the same is true of the 'provincial' nationalisms (Croats, Hungarians, Czechs) of the Habsburg empire, where the presence or absence of regional administration 'offers a much better predictor' of the rise of nations than does ethnicity (ibid.: 50).[13]

Mann, it is true, had previously offered a far more nuanced thesis about the four stages in the development of nationalism in Europe. The first stage was religious in character, starting in sixteenth-century Europe, when the Protestant Reformation and Catholic Counter-Reformation had mobilized a higher degree of 'intensive power' by encouraging new networks of elite literacy. This was followed, around 1700, by a widening of discursive literacy by commercial expansion and state militarism, which produced an upper class with a sense of 'civil citizenship'. In the third and decisive phase, from 1792, military crises turned these 'proto-nations' into real cross-class nations, albeit on a limited scale, through greater conscription, war taxes and regressive war loans, all of which made the propertied classes demand greater political representation and politicized the concepts of the 'nation' and the 'people'. In the last phase, from the late nineteenth century, industrial capitalism began to underpin nations through the agencies of an expanding state, which became responsible for a wide variety of functions; this in turn made it more representative, homogenous and 'national', and encouraged a more aggressive, fanatical nationalism (Mann 1993: 216–47).

Nevertheless, even here, Mann's emphasis falls, after the first, preparatory phase, upon the role of the state and its military and fiscal powers. The question arises as to why states should be accorded so large a nation-forming role, when Mann himself dates their first impact only after 1700, and their serious intervention no earlier than 1792. At least in the case of England, and perhaps in France, Scotland, Spain and Sweden, a sense of nationhood surely existed among both the aristocracy and the upper middle classes in the sixteenth century. To argue that these are not 'real' nations suggests that we cannot speak of nations until the late nineteenth century, when the mass of the population was first enfranchised, as Walker Connor claimed. If we are not prepared to go this far, then we may have to accept the presence of 'nations', in some sense of the term, before, and perhaps apart from, military-capitalist states.[14]

Undoubtedly, the most elaborate and trenchant statement of this general approach is the political model proposed by John Breuilly. Nationalism, for Breuilly, is best seen as a modern and purely political movement; and politics in the modern world is about control of the state. Nationalism is an argument for seizing and retaining that control. Its importance lies in its ability to offer a common platform for various sub-elites through the mobilization, coordination and legitimation of their goals and interests. Nationalist movements aim either to unify the state or to renew it or, most commonly, to oppose an existing state. As Breuilly puts it:

> [A nationalist argument] is a political doctrine built on three assertions:
> (a) There exists a nation with an explicit and peculiar character.
> (b) The interests and values of this nation take priority over all other interests and values.
> (c) The nation must be as independent as possible. This usually requires the attainment of at least political sovereignty. (Breuilly 1993: 2)

Nationalist arguments can only possess a wide appeal when modern conditions – in particular, the separation of an absolutist state from civil society – have created a sense of alienation and frustration among many educated people, who then look to doctrines that promise a reintegration of state and society. Hence the appeal of historicist arguments like those of Herder. Herder sought the rediscovery of the authentic self and the restoration of a community to its natural state, by making the cultural nation one with the political nation. Such an attempted redefinition is spurious in Breuilly's eyes, but nationalism nevertheless represented a serious attempt to address a very real problem (ibid.: 55–64).

But, in the end, ideology is only secondary to politics. It is political relations and institutions that shape the goals of nationalisms. For example, the creation of the German nation-state in 1871 had, in the end, little to do with culture and even less with Romanticism and its ideologies. It had everything to do with power politics, geopolitics and economics, especially as regards the competition between Prussia and Austria. And yet, what emerged was 'Germania' – a German nation, admittedly under the auspices of Bismarck's Prussia, but not a Prussian 'nation-state'. It was Germany that came to command the loyalty and evoke the passion of the great mass of the German-speaking population divided among so many principalities. We may be able to explain the borders created for Germany by Bismarck's *Kleindeutschland* politics, but how shall we explain the passion that, in the end, was to sweep over these borders, and the powerful identification of many ethnic Germans inside and outside those borders with a pan-German vision of 'Germania' (Breuilly 1996a)?[15]

An answer may lie within Breuilly's own definition of the first nationalist assertion, and his refusal to grant the independence movement of the United States in 1776 the title of nationalism. For Breuilly, the thirteen American colonies lacked a cultural identity – 'an explicit and peculiar character' – that could differentiate them from their mother-country and their British rulers. They were of British descent, were Christian (mainly Protestant) and spoke English, like their oppressors. But an emphasis on a cultural criterion of identity does not sit well with a purely political definition of nationalism. Similarly, Breuilly's recognition of the power of myths and ceremonial, which I mentioned in chapter 2, cannot be squared with his strictly political explanation of nationalism. And the same criticism applies to the other political modernists.[16]

We can go further. Miroslav Hroch (1985) investigated several Eastern European nationalisms, and found a common pattern of development in nationalist movements from small coteries of scholars, writers and artists elaborating the idea of the nation (phase A), to the dissemination of the idea through patriotic circles of agitators, educators and journalists (phase B), to a much wider constituency which brought in the middle and lower classes to a mass movement (phase C). Here, there is a straightforward linear development, from culture to elite politics to mass mobilization; 'culture' cannot, in these cases, be severed from 'politics'.

But the situation may be more complicated. In his detailed study of Irish nationalism and the Gaelic revival, John Hutchinson demonstrated that political nationalisms whose focus is the state and the drive for independence are regularly complemented by cultural nationalisms whose aim is the quite different one of regenerating the moral community of the nation on its own soil. Cultural nationalisms are primarily concerned with issues of cultural identity, social harmony and moral purpose; and these are concerns which for them are prior to, and independent of, any political action or expression. In practice, cultural and political forms of nationalism often succeed one another, and nationalists may oscillate between them. As a political nationalism falters in its aims, a cultural nationalism may step into the breach, building up the community's collective cultural resources; when its vigour fades, a new political movement of nationalism emerges. Nationalism, then, cannot be confined within the political, or any other, domain; and to oppose 'politics' to 'culture' or 'ethnicity' in this way does not help to advance understanding of complex phenomena such as nations and nationalism (Hutchinson 1987: ch. 1; and 1994: ch. 1).[17]

Hutchinson's wide-ranging critique touches on a second issue: the relation of culture to modernism. Movements of cultural regeneration and ethnic revival may be more common in the modern period, but they can be found in every epoch. Indeed, modern cultural nationalists need to select from pre-existing repertoires of ethnic symbols, myths and memories if they are to mobilize 'the people' to engage in the regeneration of the nation. The fact that they frequently do so suggests that

> in spite of significant differences between premodern and modern societies, long established cultural repertoires (myths, symbols and memories) are 'carried' into the modern era by powerful institutions (states, armies, churches) and are revived and redeveloped because populations are periodically faced with similar challenges to their physical and symbolic survival. (Hutchinson 2000: 661)

Once again, this addresses Breuilly's modernism, with its suspicion of retrospective nationalism and its historical scepticism vis-à-vis the persistence of cultural elements of identity from premodern periods into the modern era. For Breuilly: 'The problem with identity established outside institutions, especially those institutions which can bind people together across wide social and geographical spaces, is that it is necessarily fragmentary, discontinuous and elusive' (Breuilly 1996b: 151).

The only premodern institutions that could carry ethnic identity, the state and the church, were either threatened by national identities or were universalist. So,

> Pre-modern ethnic identity has little in the way of institutional embodiment beyond the local level. Almost all the major institutions which construct, preserve and transmit national identities, and which connect those identities to interests, are modern: parliaments, popular literature, courts, schools, labour markets, et cetera . . . National identity is essentially modern, and any useful approach to the subject must begin from this premiss. (Ibid.: 154)

This is an unnecessarily narrow, and restrictive, view of the role of institutions, culture and ethnicity in the genesis of nationalism. Many of the 'institutions' listed could be found in premodern societies. Even if they were not so inclusive as they are today, they served to 'carry' ethnic identity and culture to wider populations. Moreover, other institutions were more inclusive (and not at all fragmentary and elusive): linguistic codes, rituals and festivals, trade fairs and markets, armies and 'homelands' – all helped to instil a sense of common ethnicity over many generations and well into the modern era. 'Culture' and 'identity', once again, do not need to be severed from premodern institutions, nor need we presume a priori that they cannot furnish bases for subsequent nations.[18]

Construction and Reinterpretation

The final issue I want to consider springs directly out of the previous concerns: the extent to which nations are created *de novo* by nationalist intelligentsias or are reconstructed out of existing cultural 'materials' and ethnic sentiments.

This is a complex argument, with several facets. The idea that the nation is 'socially constructed', if it is not to be a truism, must mean something more than a simple rejection of primordialism or perennialism, for that is common to all forms of modernism. The new element here is the emphasis on social engineering and technical innovation, on the fashioning of a cultural artefact and text, on the use of skill and imagination to create novel forms. This 'strong' form of social constructionism goes beyond Gellner, for it suggests that, as they were created, so nations may, like artefacts and texts, be dissolved, and their imagining and narration may cease.

The idea that the nation is, first of all, a cultural artefact to be distinguished by the style of its *imagining* and mode of its representation, chimed with the rising tide of post-modernism, even though its original formulation emerged from a post-Marxist framework. For Benedict Anderson, nationalism is mainly a form of discourse, a type of *narrative* that imagines the political community as finite, sovereign and horizontally cross-class. Nations are based on vernacular 'print-communities', that is, reading publics of vernacular print-languages and literatures – mainly novels and newspapers, which portrayed the imagined political community in sociologically vivid and easily identifiable ways. These print-communities, in turn, were nourished by the rise of the first mass commodity, printed books, especially after the saturated elite Latin market was supplanted by the much larger vernacular markets. The growth of reading publics was aided by the Protestant ideal of scripture-reading in vernacular translations, and by the rise of centralized languages of state, which lent a sense of fixity and stability to particular languages within territorially discrete areas. Equally important, for Anderson, has been a revolution in the conception of time. Whereas in earlier periods time had been conceived as messianic and cosmological, in terms of prefiguring and fulfilment of events, now time was increasingly seen as linear and homogenous, with communities moving through an 'empty, homogenous time', and events tied to the measurements of clock and calendar (Anderson 1991: ch. 3).

Behind these early modern historical developments lay larger social changes and perennial conditions. The broad changes included the decline of sacred script communities – the great religions – and of sacred monarchical high centres

– the great empires – which left a political and cultural space for the subsequent rise of nations. Yet, ultimately, the existence of nations depends on two more perennial conditions: Babel, the fatality of global linguistic diversity, and the universal quest for an immortality that would cancel the oblivion of death. Just this immortality, to be achieved through one's posterity, through the yet unborn of the community, is what nations can confer. This is what all those 'ghostly imaginings' at the Tomb of the Unknown Warrior were about, and why this intergenerational fraternity 'makes it possible, over the past two centuries, for so many millions of people, not so much to kill, as to willingly die for such limited imaginings' (Anderson 1991: 7).[19]

Here, Anderson briefly raises the central (primordialist) problem of passion and attachment to the nation. But how does he deal with it? He claims that we are ready to sacrifice ourselves only for that which is felt to be noble and disinterested, such as the family – or the nation. But, while it is true that, as Walker Connor so vividly documented (1994: ch. 8), the nation is often likened to a family ('our family' and 'our nation'), it is not because they are pure and disinterested that families and nations elicit sacrifice. The exact reverse is the case: it is because our identities, needs and interests, our very survival, are felt to be bound up with, and dependent upon, those of 'our' family and 'our' nation, that we feel such devotion to them and are ready to sacrifice so much for them. This makes nations as much communities of emotion and will, as of imagination and cognition (Anderson 1991: 141–3; also see A. D. Smith 1998: 140–1).[20]

A similar absence of concern and scope for the role of collective will and emotion characterizes the modernist accounts propounded by Eric Hobsbawm and Terence Ranger and their associates in *The Invention of Tradition*, which appeared in the same year (1983) as the first edition of Anderson's *Imagined Communities*. For Hobsbawm, in particular, nations and nationalism owe much to the literary and historicist inventions of national history, mythology and symbolism, which flourished in Europe from about 1830 onwards, and especially after 1870. The decades before 1914 saw a flood of such 'invented traditions' – national festivals, ceremonies for the fallen, flags and anthems, statuomania, sporting contests and the like. Unlike earlier traditions, which adapted to change, the 'invented' versions were deliberate and invariant creations of cultural engineers, who forged symbols, rituals, myths and histories to meet the needs of the modern masses, whom industry and democracy were mobilizing and politicizing. In other words, they were deliberate instruments of social control by the ruling classes. Hence, says Hobsbawm, the study of invented traditions

> is highly relevant to that comparatively recent innovation, the 'nation', with its associated phenomena: nationalism, the nation-state, national symbols, histories and the rest. All these rest on exercises in social engineering that are often deliberate and always innovative, if only because historical novelty implies innovation. (Hobsbawm and Ranger 1983: 13–14)[21]

Once again, the notion of 'invention' strikes a chord in many for whom nations and nationalism are at best regrettable diversions from the 'movement of history', at worst, prime examples of the false consciousness of the masses. But, whether the nation is quite such an innovation is open to question, as is the scope for deliberate social engineering in this field. Hobsbawm's analogy here is patently mechanistic; nations are constructs or fabrications of social engineers, like technical inventions. They are planned and put together by elite craftsmen. There is no room for emotion or moral will, not even on the part of the masses. The latter are passive victims of elite social designs, which seek to channel their newly released energies. Nations and nationalism are the modern *panem et circenses* (ibid.: ch. 7).

But are the masses simply a *tabula rasa*, waiting for the nationalist messages of their rulers to be inscribed on their minds and hearts? Hobsbawm is aware of the problem of an exclusively 'top-down' approach, but his solution is to reject in advance any links between the 'proto-national bonds' of the masses, whether regional, religious or linguistic, and modern nationalisms in search of independent territorial states. He concedes that in premodern periods we can find many 'proto-national' communities based on regional languages and local religions, but he argues that these cannot be the ancestors or progenitors of nations because 'they had or have no *necessary* relation with the unit of territorial political organisation which is a crucial criterion of what we understand as a "nation" today' (Hobsbawm 1990: 47; italics in original).

The few exceptions, like England and France, Russia and Serbia, are cases where a great institution (the state or church) has survived, or the memory of a lasting political community has persisted into the modern epoch and provides the basis for a subsequent mass nationalism. Any other historical link is spurious, for it operates beyond what Hobsbawm terms 'effective historical continuity' (Hobsbawm and Ranger 1983: 7; also see Hobsbawm 1990: ch. 2).

But is it so spurious? And what exactly is 'effective historical continuity'? Besides, does it really matter for the creation of nations? Objective historicity may be important in the long run, but for the mass of the population a narrative must have emotive 'resonance' as much as 'truth-content'. This is a central theoretical consideration for ethno-symbolists like myself. What matters for an explanation of the power and durability of nations and nationalism is that the narratives and images of the nation strike a chord with the people to whom they are designed to appeal; and that 'the people' and their cultures can, in turn, contribute to the process of reconstructing the nation. Only when they can 're-present' to the mass of the population an acceptable and inspiring image or narrative of the nation can elites exert any influence and provide some leadership.

Central to this argument is the relationship between cognition and emotion. If we are to grasp the deep hold and wide appeal of nationalism, we cannot proceed from purely cognitive or interest-based models. We need to understand nationalism as a type of collective conduct, based on the collective will of a moral community and the shared emotions of a putatively ancestral community; and this means that we need to grasp the nation as a political form of the sacred community of citizens. Though Anderson concedes the linguistic basis of the imagined political community, and though he touches briefly on the deeper, religious grounds for national identity, he fails to develop its affective, let alone its moral, potential. Instead, he sees the nation through the cognitive lens of its intellectual and artistic purveyors, in terms of the concept of 'imagination'. In the same manner, though Hobsbawm concedes the importance for nationalists of deep historical continuity, he regards their narratives as spurious, and thereby excludes the possibility of grasping their emotional appeal. The latter has nothing to do with their 'innovative' qualities, let alone their truth-content, and everything to do with the traditions of popular ethnic myths, symbols and memories which nationalisms habitually evoke, and invoke. To dismiss or ignore these is to preclude a deeper understanding of the popular bases of nations and nationalism.

That is why ethno-symbolists, whom I briefly introduced at the end of chapter 3, have seen the process of nation-formation as not so much one of construction, let alone deliberate 'invention', as of *reinterpretation* of pre-existing cultural motifs and of *reconstruction* of earlier ethnic ties and sentiments. If modernists and constructionists have been overly concerned with a 'retrospective nationalism', ethno-symbolists have pointed to the equally serious dangers of a 'blocking presentism', that is, an exclusive focus on the views and interests of the present generation in shaping the past. This makes it difficult, if not impossible, to grasp the many ways in which ethnic pasts help to shape present concerns by providing the cultural frameworks and parameters within and through which the needs and understandings of the present are formed and articulated. Besides being historically shallow, the presentist view simply does not stand up to historical scrutiny. There has never been a *tabula rasa* (see Peel 1989; A. D. Smith 1998: ch. 8).

For ethno-symbolists like Armstrong, Hutchinson and myself, nations and nationalism can only be understood through an analysis of collective cultural identities over *la longue durée*. But the connections of the past to the present and future can never constitute a single one-way causal relationship; there are different kinds of links, depending on external circumstances and the resources of the community (see Armstrong 1982 and 1995; Hutchinson 1994; A. D. Smith 1986 and 1999a: Introduction).

As a start, we might distinguish three such relationships – of cultural continuity, recurrence and reinterpretation. *Continuity* can be found in such components as collective proper names, language codes and ethnic landscapes, all of which may linger on, even after the community to which they were attached has all but vanished, as occurred in the case of the Punic culture of the Carthaginians, some five centuries after the total destruction of Carthage by the Romans. But they may also provide the framework for the revival of the community in a new form, after many vicissitudes and transformations; the Greeks afford a good example of this revival and reidentification through continuity of names, language and landscapes.[22]

Recurrence of *ethnies* and nations is more complex. This is not just a matter of tracing back the roots of particular nations to the medieval epoch and beyond, but of demonstrating that the national form of collective cultural identity and community recurs in other epochs and continents, and may therefore continue to do so in the future. In other words, the concept of the nation refers to a type of cultural resource and of human association that is potentially available in all periods of history. This type of linkage between past, present and future comes close to the perennialist claim. Yet it differs from it in acknowledging historical breaks, the ruptures in continuity both between different nations in the same area and between the national forms taken by the self-same community in the same or different areas. So, we may witness the emergence of nations along with *ethnies* in a particular area, say, in the Hellenistic Near East, followed by their decline and dissolution and the rise of other nations, say, in medieval Europe or the Far East. We could also show the extent to which particular *ethnies*, such as the Armenians or Jews in late antiquity, approximated the national form of community, the subsequent shedding or 'loss' of that national form and its re-emergence or re-acquisition in the modern period. From this standpoint, nations are recurrent, but not continuous, features of human society and politics. These are questions to which I shall return.

Finally, and less controversially, the relationship between past, present and future may be one of *reinterpretation*. Here, intellectuals and leaders of aspirant communities seek to rediscover their 'authentic' history and link them with putative 'golden ages' in their ethnic pasts, in order to regenerate them and restore their 'glorious destiny'. They do so by selecting and reinterpreting for each generation the meanings of these pasts within the parameters of that ethnic culture, sifting the genuine elements from the inauthentic, the intrinsic from the extraneous. If the relationship in these cases is overtly ideological, it nevertheless possesses the power to mobilize large numbers of people and imbue them with a sense of collective purpose on behalf of what is felt to 'their own' community, as many examples testify. The resort to the ethnic past, however tenuous, can inspire in 'the people' a desire and will to self-sacrifice for co-nationals which few ideologies can match. It can also furnish a comprehensive framework for understanding the place of the individual in the community and world, as well as a distinctive outlook and programme for the nation as a whole.[23]

It follows that, in contrast to the constructionist outlook, ethno-symbolic approaches insist on the need to place the rise of modern nations in the context of previous collective cultural identities in premodern epochs. The most important type among these communities is the *ethnie*, the named human population which is associated with a particular territory, and which shares myths of ancestry and historical memories, as well as elements of common culture. This is the social formation that is generally ignored by constructionists, and by modernists as a whole; and it is one that is elided by perennialism. There is, perhaps, a hint of recognition of its importance in Anderson's references to language as the criterion of community ('from the start the nation was conceived in language, not in blood' (1991: 145)), and Kedourie appears to accept as self-evident the ethnic diversity of humanity and the problems this causes when nationalism infects ethnically mixed areas. But, in general, the story told by modernists is historically truncated, a post-Revolutionary tale of progressive modernity sweeping away the vestiges of the past and its patchwork of ethnic and religious cultures, whereas, for ethno-symbolists, the nation is inconceivable outside of a world of ethnicity, and particular nations are unlikely to emerge except on the basis of prior ethnic ties. While this does not mean that for every nation there must have been a prior *ethnie* serving as its sole basis – for very few nations are not ethnically diverse – it does mean that nations are specialized developments of (one or more) looser ethnic groups and that the ethnic community has historically served as the model and basis of many nations. Failure to recognize the implications of this fact has, in my view, seriously hampered the development of the study of nations and nationalism, as has the concomitant lack of attention to the ethnic memories, myths, symbols and traditions that provide such vital clues to the understanding – and persistence – of cultural identities and communities (A. D. Smith 1986 and 1999a; cf. Kedourie 1960: ch. 6)[24]

Conclusion

These, then, are some of the main lines of discussion and debate that have taken place in the last three decades of the twentieth century in the field of ethnicity and nationalism. Of course, they do not exhaust the debates or cover all of the major theoretical works. It is impossible in a short book to do justice to all the arguments, let alone research, in this rapidly proliferating field. Some of the more recent debates, notably about the hybridization of nations and the effects of globalization, I shall consider in the last chapter. But, even these more recent developments can only be understood in the context of the 'paradigm debates' that I have discussed above. These provide the foundations and frameworks within which subsequent arguments have been conducted. As I shall argue, the most recent debates are essentially outgrowths of the earlier approaches, rather than marking any new paradigm break.

Not only are these recent theoretical debates essentially developments of earlier approaches, they also presuppose certain historiographies of the nation and nationalism, and rest on their underlying paradigms. We need to describe and comprehend the various 'histories of the nation' offered by the rival approaches, not only for their own sakes, but for the insight they afford for grasping recent theoretical debates and the empirical prospects of nationalism. To these histories I now turn.

5
Histories

There is a widely accepted 'history of nationalism', and it is one that is decidedly modernist.

It starts in the last quarter of the eighteenth century, from the Partitions of Poland and the American Revolution through the French Revolution to the reaction to Napoleon's conquests in Prussia, Russia and Spain. Nationalism, according to this view, was born during these forty years of revolution. Subsequently, it spread in fits and starts to other parts of Europe – Serbia, Greece, Poland (again) – as well as among the creole elites of Latin America, from 1810 to the 1820s. The first great wave of nationalisms culminated in the 1848 Revolutions in Europe – the so-called 'spring of peoples' – and its main achievements were the unification of Germany and Italy, under Prussian and Piedmontese auspices, and the elevation of Hungary within the Habsburg empire. In the latter third of the nineteenth century, a second wave of nationalisms burgeoned in Eastern and Northern Europe – Czech, Slovak, Romanian, Bulgarian, Lithuanian, Finnish, Norwegian, Jewish – along with a few nationalisms outside Europe – in Meiji Japan, India, Armenia and Egypt. The latter were soon joined in the first decades of the twentieth century by a variety of ethnic nationalisms in Asia – Turkish, Arab, Persian, Burman, Javanese, Filippino, Vietnamese and Chinese – and the first stirrings of nationalisms in Africa – in Nigeria, Ghana and South Africa. By the 1930s and 1940s, there was hardly a corner of the globe that had not been touched by the nationalist onslaught, while the same period saw the apogee of nationalism in Europe, culminating in Nazism and the genocide of the Second World War, on the one hand, and the subsequent anti-colonial 'liberation' nationalisms in Africa and Asia.[1]

There is an uneasy coda to this story. When it was widely assumed that it had 'spent its force', nationalism seemed to spring to life once again in the movements for ethnic autonomy in the West in the 1960s and 1970s – in Catalonia and ꞌ ꞏdi, Corsica and Brittany, Flanders, Scotland and ꞏ   ꞏ Quebec – only to die down, apparently, in   hen be revived, when *perestroika* and *glas-*   he nationalisms of the titular republics of   ꞏer 1988, which in turn contributed to the   ꞏet Union in 1991. In this heady atmos-   we have witnessed new tragedies of   ꞏe last decade of the twentieth century   tinent, in the Middle East and the   ꞏla, in the Caucasus, above all, in the   ꞏuncertain aftermath.

'Gre ꞏ Nations', Small *Ethnies*

I have outlined the basic sequence of the many modernist histories and typologies of nationalism, conceived as a modern ideology and movement. In some cases, the tale embodies a moral of hubris and nemesis: the first phase of gestation produced a romantic upsurge, which led to an aggressive nationalism of the great powers after 1871, followed by the catastrophes of two world wars and the dissipation of nationalism. However, as the time-scale lengthened, and nationalism failed to fade away, this simple cautionary tale had to be revised. That, in turn, meant abandoning a single, linear model for a much more pluralist, and geoculturally diverse, approach, in which the elites of each global area, while 'pirating the patent' (of the original European product), in Anderson's words, assimilated it to the needs and problems of their own societies and cultures (see Anderson 1991: chs 4–9).[2]

Nevertheless, the appeal of a unitary model remains strong, embodying as it does the influence of approaches derived from the modernist paradigm. One such approach, which has become influential, is the constructionist model of 'invented (national) traditions'. As I explained, this is a model of social engineering and social control, in which Western elites channel and shape the activities and sentiments of the newly enfranchised masses in an age of industrial capitalism and democratization. This is the approach adopted by Eric Hobsbawm in his rich and detailed history of two kinds of nationalism.

Hobsbawm, as we saw in chapter 4, regards nationalism as a strictly modern political movement, whose aim is the creation of territorial states. This means that, as historians, we cannot trace the ideology of nationalism further back than the French Revolution. Yet, curiously, Hobsbawm's history begins not in 1780, as the title of his 1990 book proclaims, but in 1830, after the July Revolution in Paris, when the citizen-nation of the French Revolution was re-established and when we can see a growing bourgeois-democratic resistance to the Metternichian Settlement of 1815. That was when the 'great nations' were fully formed, first in Britain and France, and subsequently by Germany and Italy, nations whose outstanding characteristics were the extent of their territory and the size of their population. These, according to Hobsbawm, provided a 'threshold principle' for legitimating nationhood and statehood. Following the ideas of Friedrich List, it was generally accepted (even by the likes of Mazzini) that only those nations which achieved this threshold of territorial extent, demographic size and economic (market) strength, could plausibly hope to be admitted to the comity of states. From 1830 to 1870, according to Hobsbawm, the threshold principle held sway, and it meant that the 'principle of nationality' 'applied in practice only to nationalities of a certain size', for only large nations were viable, economically and culturally (Hobsbawm 1990: 30–2).[3]

It also meant that great nation nationalism had to have a unifying, inclusive and expansionist character. In the eyes of liberals, this was the direction in which history was moving: towards ever larger units of territory, population and resources. By the same token, the nationalisms of the great nations were mainly civic and mass-democratic in character, for they aimed to include ever larger numbers of the national population as citizens in the political arena, taking as their model the constitutions approved during the French Revolution.[4]

Hobsbawm is very much aware of the governmental, or 'top-down,' nature of this approach, and he is at pains to correct it by including in his analysis the many popular 'proto-national' communities of language, region and religion which often formed among the mass of the population in premodern epochs. Yet, as we saw in the last chapter, these communities play little or no part in the unfolding drama of nationalism. Having criticized Gellner for failing to take popular sentiments and ties into account, Hobsbawm in effect follows Gellner in dividing the mass of the population into discrete cultural groups which cannot serve as springboards for the construction of nations, because they are too localized and, in most cases, apolitical. The few exceptions are cases where a proto-nationalism of the people was identified with a medieval state and church, as in England, Serbia or Russia, and this continuing identification was able to facilitate the growth of a modern political nationalism. Thus 'membership of a historic (or actual) state present or past, can act directly upon the consciousness of the common people to produce proto-nationalism – or perhaps even, as in the case of Tudor England, something close to modern patriotism' (Hobsbawm 1990: 75). And, in the case of the Serbs, it was the tradition of an early state that served modern Serb nationalism, for the memory of the 'old kingdom defeated by the Turks was preserved in song and heroic story, and perhaps more to the point, in the daily liturgy of the Serbian church which had canonised most of its kings' (ibid.: 76).

Hence, as with Renan and Weber, political memories and institutions are held to be potent over *la longue durée*, while ethnic and linguistic identification are seen as modern and contrived. This sounds very much like another version of Hegel's theory of 'historyless peoples', the view that only those peoples who had forged a political tradition of statecraft in the past would be able to build modern nations and national states in the future (see Rosdolsky 1964).

That would certainly fit with Hobsbawm's negative view of the later development of nationalism in Europe. For he contends that, after the first great age of European nationalism, from 1830 to 1870, which was inclusive, civic and democratic, a second type of nationalism swept Eastern Europe, characterized by an appeal to ethnicity or language, or both. But, for Hobsbawm, ethnicity and language are ambiguous concepts and neither can provide clear-cut criteria for nationhood. This second kind of nationalism, explains Hobsbawm, differed from the first in three ways:

> First, it abandoned the 'threshold principle' which, as we have seen, was so central in the Liberal era. Henceforth *any* body of people considering themselves a 'nation' claimed the right to self-determination which, in the last analysis, meant the right to a separate sovereign independent state for their territory. Second, and in consequence of this multiplication of potential 'unhistorical' nations, ethnicity and language became the central, increasingly the decisive and even the only criteria of potential nationhood. Yet there was a third change which affected not so much the nation-state national movements, but national sentiments within the established nation-states: a sharp shift to the political right of nation and flag, for which the term 'nationalism' was actually invented in the last decade(s) of the nineteenth century. (Hobsbawm 1990: 102; emphasis in original)

This period, 1870–1914, saw the proliferation of ethno-linguistic nationalisms in Europe, together with a rapid expansion of the franchise consequent on an explosion of urban industrialism. It was also an age of rising new classes and ethnic migration, and of mass racist xenophobia, directed mainly by the lower middle classes ('the lesser examination-passing classes') against foreigners, and especially the Jews (ibid.: 109–11, 121, 133).

This period and type of nationalism reached its apogee in mid-twentieth-century racial fascism and Nazism. After 1945, and a period of relative quiescence, there has been a revival of the divisive and fissiparous ethno-linguistic nationalisms which are the heirs of the late nineteenth-century small-nationality nationalisms. But there is an important difference. Nationalism today 'is no longer a major vector of historical development'. Rather, ethnic nationalisms appear as 'reactions of weakness and fear, attempts to erect barricades to keep at bay the forces of the modern world', in which massive global economic transformations and population movements disorient and frighten many people. Today, nationalism has become irrelevant. It has lost its former state-making and economy-forming functions, and has become a 'substitute for lost dreams' (ibid.: 164, 175–6, 181).

Hobsbawm concludes on a hopeful note: 'The owl of Minerva which brings wisdom, said Hegel, flies out at dusk. It is a good sign that it is now circling round nations and nationalism' (ibid.: 183).

Nations Before Nationalism

I have cited Hobsbawm's account at some length, both because it has become so influential, but even more because it embodies so clearly the main features of the constructionist version of a modernist paradigm. These include:

(1) the view that nationalism, along with the modern state, created nations;
(2) that nations, like nationalism, are no older than the early nineteenth century;
(3) that nations and nationalism itself are artefacts of the intelligentsia and bourgeoisie;
(4) that ethnic ('ethno-linguistic') nationalisms need to be distinguished from civic-political nationalisms;
(5) that nationalism and nations have fulfilled their functions and are now becoming obsolete in an era of globalization.[5]

But these modernist views of the nature, periodization and role of nations and nationalism have come in for some heavy criticism. Each of Hobsbawm's modernist contentions has been challenged. I shall return to the last contention, the possible obsolescence of nations and nationalism, in the next chapter. For the moment I want to consider the others in turn.

Nations as products of nationalism?

Because nationalism is widely seen as a modern ideology, the idea that it creates nations assumes not only that there were no nations before nationalism, but that there can be no pre-nationalist nations. More than this, it assumes that 'nations' constitute a form of discourse and a cultural artefact, which are constructs that can only acquire meaning within a wider ideology of nationalism. The argument here is that earlier meanings of the term 'nation' are necessarily quite different from, and have no connection with, the modern (post-1789) nationalism-dependent meanings.

Quite apart from the question of the relation of 'words' to 'things', there are actually two problems here. The first is that the modern meanings of the term 'nation' are varied and often ambiguous. We have only to refer to the many differences among scholars themselves as to the meanings of the term; and the same holds true for political participants and the general public. In different parts of the world, different criteria are used to define what people mean by the term; these include religion, language and customs, ethnicity, territory and statehood, singly or in combinations. As we have seen, the various nationalist ideologies frame quite different concepts of the nation, within the overall 'nationalist family'. From which, then, of these modern meanings, do earlier meanings of the term 'nation' differ so much?[6]

The second problem is more serious. Even assuming we could fix a single, acceptable meaning for the term today, how can we be sure that earlier (say, medieval) meanings of 'nation' differ that much from modern ones? This is a point explored by Adrian Hastings. Hastings claims that the English case demonstrates a broad continuity of meaning for the term 'nation' from the fourteenth century onwards. Words such as 'nacion' (Fortescue) or 'nacyon' (Fabian) in the fifteenth century, and 'nacioun' (Wyclif and Rolle) in the fourteenth, are used in much the same sense as more recent usages, such as Milton's in his *Areopagitica* of 1644

('Methinks I see in my mind a noble and puissant nation raising herself like a strong man after sleep') or Samuel Johnson in his *Dictionary* of 1755, where a nation is defined as 'A people distinguished from another people; generally by their language, origin, or government', or Pitt the Younger's appeal to 'our existence as a nation ... our very name as Englishmen'. All this suggests that, from the early fourteenth century at least, 'Englishmen felt themselves to be a nation' (Hastings 1997: 14–16).

One important reason for this consistency of usage was the many English translations of the Vulgate version of the Bible, from Rolle and Wyclif, augmented after the Reformation by the weekly readings from the Book of Common Prayer. Where the Vulgate had translated the Greek 'ethnos' as 'natio', the English used the words 'nacioun' or 'nacion', and later 'nation'. And the word 'natio' was 'regularly used in the Middle Ages in the Vulgate sense of a people distinct by "language, laws, habits, modes of judgment and customs" – to use an almost defining phrase of Bernard, first Norman Bishop of St David's, when describing the Welsh as a "natio" to the Pope about 1140' (ibid.: 17). Hastings concludes from this brief linguistic excursus than in the English language, at least, there has been 'a surprisingly firm continuity in usage across more than six hundred years', one that has deep biblical and Vulgate roots – and to disregard such widespread usage and use the term 'natio' to refer only to the divisions of students in medieval universities is absurd (ibid.: 17–18).[7]

Of course, 'words' are not the same as 'things'. But, if the sentiment of belonging to a nation is to count as one of the criteria of nationhood, then, in the English case, at least, there is a *prima facie* case for saying that 'nations precede nationalism', because of this consistency of linguistic usage and the underlying conviction of national belonging which it expresses.

Modernists might respond by arguing that even if in a few cases the nation appears to be older than (its) nationalism, most nations are the product of national*ism* and require the cognitive model of the nation propounded by nationalist ideology, *together with* the activism of the nationalist ideal of self-determination. Moreover, what distinguishes the modern, or 'real', nation, is the rise of citizenship: nations are mass phenomena in which, according to nationalist ideology, every member of the nation is *ipso facto* a citizen. And only in the modern period does citizenship become widely available.[8]

Against these objections, Hastings points (again, through the English case) to the 'nationalism' of medieval nations. Though they lacked a *theory* of nationalism, these nations displayed a clear and active nationalism of their own, especially under threat and during conflicts. For Hastings, nationalism is really a particularistic movement. This is the source of its strength, not some general theory of self-determination. It may well be that, from 1800 onwards, many nations were preceded and shaped by nationalism (the ideology). But, before that date, it was the other way round: nations under threat produced their own nationalisms, and were as 'self-determining' as the post-1789 'Mark II' variety of nations.

Premodern nations?

For Hastings, modernism tells only one half of the story of nationalism; the other, the pre-1789 half, has been omitted.

The neo-perennialist story advanced by Hastings is a selective one, but its thrust is to deny the linkage between nations, nationalism and modernity on which Hobsbawm and other modernists insist, and to demonstrate the identity and continuity of certain nations from their premodern beginnings to their present manifestations. Hastings' choices are predominantly West European, and especially British: England, first, followed by Scotland, Ireland and Wales; then France, Holland, Switzerland, Sweden, Germany and Spain. This is very much in the tradition of Hugh Seton-Watson, who distinguished the 'old, continuous' nations from the newly created nations, mainly in Eastern Europe and Asia, after 1800: 'The old nations of Europe in 1789 were the English, Scots, French, Dutch, Castilians and Portuguese in the west; the Danes and Swedes in the north; and the Hungarians, Poles and Russians in the east' (Seton-Watson 1977: 7).

In these cases, the nation grew spontaneously, that is, it was not willed into existence by nationalist or other elites. Such nations lacked a nationalist blueprint or design – in

Hastings' terms, a nationalist theory. But, they were nonetheless nations – and 'nationalist', at that.[9]

Overall, Hastings' version of continuous perennialism distinguishes 'three large stages of development' of European national identities. The first is 'that of a mass of local ethnicities, many of them of a fairly unstable sort', from the fifth to the fourteenth century, depending upon region. These were largely oral ethnicities; but in a few cases, the spoken language was committed to writing, and a vernacular literature began to fix the boundaries of emergent nations. By the fifteenth century, and the second stage, the development of literary languages and large states had diminished the complexity and fluidity of the ethnic map, and

> most of the main nations of western Europe can be seen to exist. People regularly spoke of them as such. They are precisely the same nations produced by nationalisms from the late eighteenth century on, according to the theorists of modernism. The correlation is so close that it would be absurd to regard it as accidental. (Hastings 1997: 114)

The third stage in the development of nationhood, 'misleadingly regarded by modernists as its total history', began in the late eighteenth century with the collapse of the French monarchy, which 'opened the floodgates to revolutionary movements that were also nationalist' (ibid.: 119). This is the period of nations created by nationalism, on which modernists focus, but it is less the result of 'modernization' than of the influence of the successful English civic and parliamentary model, notably in France.[10]

For neo-perennialists like Hastings, then, there *can* be premodern nations, and most of them were to be found in Western Europe, following the English prototype. And Hastings is not alone in this assessment. John Gillingham, too, regards England as a nation even before the fourteenth century. In the work of William of Malmesbury and Geoffrey of Monmouth, as well as of Giraldus Cambrensis, in the eleventh and twelfth centuries, we find clear enunciations of a sense of English nationhood, in opposition to the Welsh and Irish; this, despite the Angevin possession of territories in

France, which can be seen as an early example of 'English imperialism' (Gillingham 1992).

Similarly, Josep Llobera, while insisting on the relative modernity of nationalist ideology, locates the bases of later nations in the long history of ethnic and political ties and sentiments in key areas of Europe such as 'Francia', 'Germania' and 'Hispania'. Without analysing the terrain and memories provided by such cultural-political formations, we can never hope to explain the subsequent emergence of the familiar modern political nations (Llobera 1994: Part I).[11]

So, against a modernist like John Breuilly, for whom the growth of national sentiment in the sixteenth century is no more than a 'prelude' to nationalism, neo-perennialists argue for the existence of nations and nationalisms even before the sixteenth century. Of course, the Reformation, with its emphasis on individual prayer and Bible-reading in vernacular translations, greatly enhanced and diffused the feelings of nationhood, a point made in rich detail in Liah Greenfeld's great study of the main nationalist routes to modernity. Indeed, for Greenfeld, English nationalism slightly antedated the Reformation. For the feeling that the nation was identical with the whole people – in her opinion the key criterion of the presence of nationalism – first became widespread among the English elite in the 1520s and 1530s. But the Protestant English Bible and Book of Common Prayer, together with Foxe's book of (Protestant) *Martyrs*, gave that national sentiment a huge boost and a potent cause, against the Roman Church and its Spanish ally. By the time of the Armada, a sense of English nationhood had spread to the middle classes in most areas, and it provided the model for subsequent nationalisms in France, Germany, Russia and the United States (Greenfeld 1992: ch. 1).[12]

The sources of nationalism

In the neo-perennialist account, the sources of national identities are to be sought in popular sentiments and culture, and not primarily in the imaginations and inventions of elites. Nations cannot, therefore, be explained as modern artefacts fashioned by contending elites. Though elites play important roles, the fundamental sources of nations and national identity must be located elsewhere, and much further back in time.

For Adrian Hastings, as we saw, premodern nations are formed from fluid ethnicities through the development of literary languages and of literatures which fix the boundaries of cultures and peoples. No doubt, premodern 'intellectuals' – poets, scribes and priests – played vital roles here. But for Hastings, the main source of nationalism is religion, and more specifically Christianity. Not only did it provide the main educational and social welfare networks, but its clergy were in daily contact with the mass of villagers, and, through its weekly sermons and readings, the Church exerted a powerful influence over the emotions and outlook of the masses. Moreover, the Church had sanctioned the use of vernacular languages; with the result that the message it preached was as much national as universal, because, alongside the Gospel, the Church had adopted the Old Testament and its political ideal of sacred nationality and kingship. Even while it repudiated the people of the Book, the Church, lacking in the Gospels the model of an ideal polity, had accepted the Jewish prototype of the nation of Israel, seeing itself as the true Israel (*verus Israel*), and the heir of God's chosen people. The resultant message was simple: every nation could be God's chosen people, a nation like the ancient Jews, provided it was truly Christian and faithful to the Church. (Hastings 1997: chs 1, 9).[13]

Hence, it is to literature and the clergy, the Church and biblical religion, that we must look for the origins and development of nationalism. Without Christianity and, before it, Judaism, there could be neither nations nor nationalism.

A similar conclusion can be drawn from Conor Cruse O'Brien's (1988a) analysis of the nature and origins of 'holy nationalism' and its deification of the people, which goes back to the unified vision of biblical territorialism, of ethnic community and promised land conjoined with religion recorded in the Old Testament. O'Brien goes on to show how this tradition took hold in Europe, and has found new expression in the sacred character of American nationalism with its saluting of the flag and its prayer meetings.

For neo-perennialists, then, the sources of nations and nationalism must be sought not in the blueprints of secular intelligentsias nor in the interests of the middle classes in the modern epoch, but in the 'deep cultural resources' of language, ethnicity and religion. This conclusion makes it far easier to accept the ideas both of 'nations before nationalism' and 'nations before modernity'. In fact, it can lead to a questioning of Hastings' tripartite schema from the other end, as it were, of the historical spectrum, suggesting the possibility of nations and nationalism in antiquity, something that Hastings himself alludes to when he notes the existence of isolated nations in Armenia and Ethiopia, before England – and, of course, in ancient Israel itself. This is an issue to which I shall return.[14]

The ubiquity and durability of these deep cultural resources also calls into question the Eurocentric approach of both perennialists and modernists, for it opens up a debate about the presence of premodern nations outside Europe, particularly in Iran and the Far East. For Hastings, nationalism came to Asia from Europe through Christianity and colonialism. He does not appear to consider the possibility that, on his own criteria, Japan, Korea and China, as well as Pagan Burma and Safavid Persia, already constituted nations in the medieval epoch. After all, they possessed vernacular languages and literatures, as well as myths of unique origins and common descent. Moreover, their polities were supported by powerful religious institutions and ideals. The model of the polity in Confucianism, let alone Buddhism, may not be so dynamic and strenuous as that of ancient Israel adopted by Christianity (or, for that matter, of Islam), and in that sense, Hastings may be able to help us explain why nationalist *ideology* originated in the West, and why the Reformation, with its return to the Old Testament Hebrews, helped to consolidate the first wave of Western nations. But, if we adopt Hastings' criteria of nationhood, and his periodization of national development in the West, then we shall also have to concede the presence of nations in Asia in the self-same medieval epoch.[15]

Ethnic and civic nations

For the modernists and constructionists, ethnic nationalism is best understood as a naturalized form of elite invention. It

is a political version of 'fictive ethnicity'. In the words of
Etienne Balibar and Immanuel Wallerstein:

> No nation possesses an ethnic base naturally, but as social
> formations are nationalised, the populations included within
> them, divided up among them or dominated by them are eth-
> nicised – that is, represented in the past or in the future *as if*
> they formed a natural community, possessing of itself an iden-
> tity of origins, culture and interests which transcend individ-
> uals and social conditions. (Balibar and Wallerstein 1991: 96;
> emphasis in original)[16]

We found the same deconstructionist emphasis in Hobsbawm's critical questioning of the nature and role of language
and ethnicity in the creation of modern nations, by comparison with the (temporary) economic and political necessity of
large civic nations. But, for perennialists in general, it is the
other way round: civic nationalism, or patriotism, in Walker
Connor's terminology, is, if not artificial, certainly a rational
construct, whereas ethnic nationalism, rooted as it is, ultimately, in felt kinship ties, is congruent with the basic emotions generated by human experience and family relations. It
follows that nations, if not 'natural', are based upon ethnicity and ethno-linguistic ties, however much support a particular nation may have received from its state.

This is a point that Hastings underlines in the Irish and,
to a lesser extent, the Welsh cases. Here, despite the shadowy
High Kings of Ireland and Brian Boru, and a brief period of
unity in much of Wales before the English conquest, the state
played a minimal role in defining the nation. Ireland was
defined by its religious history, starting with St Patrick's
mission, and by its island geography and holy sites, as an
insula sacra. This is supported by James Lydon's account of
the clear distinction drawn in the medieval epoch between the
Irish and the English in Ireland, for example in the 'remon-
strance' of 1317 or the Statutes of Kilkenny of 1366, with
their cultural and quasi-racial stereotypes, well before the
Reformation and the Protestant Scots settlement in Ireland.
A similar distinction was manifest between the Welsh and the
English, symbolized by the name of *Cymry* and, further back,
by the myth of (Roman) Britain. These are longstanding

ethnic nationalisms, and ethnicity forms their basis, as it does of most of today's nationalisms, whether in the former Yugoslavia or the Caucasus or in Africa (Hastings 1997: chs 3, 5, 6; Lydon 1995).[17]

From a neo-perennialist standpoint, the distinction drawn between 'ethnic' and 'civic' nations and nationalisms, so fashionable today, is at best secondary, at worst misleading. In effect, all nations and their nationalisms are, at root, 'ethnic', historically speaking; and though the nation may in time come to transcend a given ethnicity and incorporate other *ethnies* within a broader political community, it derives its mobilizing power from the shared conviction of its unique ancestry and history. This does not make the ethnic base in any way 'natural'; but neither is it an interpretation or imposition of nationalists. Rather, it is to recognize in ethnicity, language and religion the historical and structural bases of nationhood, and the socio-historical contexts of particular nations. Modernists, committed to a West European and American focus and perspective, have treated the territorially based political communities of the modern West as the canonical nations – whereas in fact they are really only special cases of formerly ethnic nations fostered by strong states and transmuted over the centuries into more territorially based nations and political nationalisms.[18]

This is a view that receives some support from the fact that Western states were historically formed around 'ethnic cores' – dominant *ethnies* which originated or founded the community and supplied most of the elite personnel of the state, as was the case in the first national states – England, France, Holland, Spain and Sweden – as well as in Hungary, Poland and Muscovite Russia. Even an immigrant nation like the United States was created by the elites of a dominant Protestant British *ethnie*, although its ethnic character was subsequently transformed by waves of immigrants on a large scale. Over the centuries, these strong states expanded territorially and annexed different regions and their peoples, while preserving the position of the dominant *ethnie* well into the twentieth century (see A. D. Smith 1989).

In these cases, the 'ethnic–civic' dichotomy is historically inaccurate and sociologically misleading. These are ethnic nations that have been gradually transformed into more territorially based and multicultural political communities. The contrast between territory and genealogy, between *ius soli* and *ius sanguinis*, which Rogers Brubaker uses to illuminate the differences between French and German immigration and citizenship policies and practices, must not be overdrawn. Most nations exemplify both principles of social organization, even if they choose to emphasize one of them over the other at any given time (Brubaker 1992; cf. Schnapper 1997).

Nations in Antiquity?

If the tripartite scheme of national development proposed by Hastings – an early medieval epoch of oral ethnicities, a later medieval/early modern epoch of Mark I nations, and a modern era of ideologically driven Mark II nations – can be criticized for its Eurocentrism, it can also be questioned for its neglect of earlier epochs of human history. With one exception, Hastings fails to apply his criteria to antiquity, or consider the possibility of nations before or outside the Judaeo-Christian tradition. If a vernacular literature, supported by geography and statehood, is the main criterion of nationhood, as it is in the English case, how can we include the Israelites and exclude the ancient Egyptians, Babylonians or Persians? Granted that a Christianity based on the Bible was an important factor in disseminating the idea of the nation in Europe and the Americas, why should we accord it priority over those ethno-linguistic criteria that would encourage us to discern the character of 'nations' in other, earlier communities?

This is where the emphasis on continuity of most perennialists comes in. Hastings and others might well be prepared to allow the title of nation to other communities in antiquity, but they lack historical significance because they were isolated instances and they did not survive as nations – whereas England has not only been a continuous nation from at least the fourteenth century, but has spawned a whole series of other continuous nations. Egypt, Persia, Assyria, even Greece, 'died' as nations, without progeny, but England stood at the head of the great column of nations.[19]

To this generalization there was, of course, one great exception: the Jews. They constituted the original ideal and prototype of the nation, and yet, for Hastings, they had 'lost' their nationhood for nearly two thousand years and have only now recovered it in Israel. This is puzzling, because on Hastings' own criteria of nationhood – namely (1) an ethnicity, (2) fixed in a vernacular language and literature, and (3) modelled on the biblical prototype – the Jews, even in their diaspora or Exile (*Galut*), remained pre-eminently a continuous nation, a highly literate people with a sacred language and literature, which they continually rehearsed and augmented in their diaspora, while remaining faithful to their covenant and promised land.[20]

Clearly, another criterion is operative here: residence in and possession of a homeland territory. This is undoubtedly an important criterion of nationhood, and historically often decisive, as well as vital to nationalist ideology. Whether in the future 'nations' may be conceived as deterritorialized communities is a question I shall consider in the next chapter. But such a formulation concedes the norm of territoriality for nationhood: in the past, the nation has always been seen as a territorial community.[21]

But, if territory is vital to nationhood, what better example of a nation than the ancient Egyptians? Confined to a narrow slither of territory on the banks of the Nile, with deserts on either side and their closest neighbours – Nubians and Asiatics – clearly differentiated from them in customs, religion, language and physiognomy, possessing, moreover, an all-pervasive unified religion and powerful state, and (in the Hymn of Akhnaton, for example) clearly perceiving their difference from other nations and languages, what reason can there be for denying the ancient Egyptians the title of 'nation' and indeed of 'national state'? (see Trigger et al. 1983).

Modernists may object that ancient Egypt was an isolated instance; it was not part of a system of national states, which is an indispensable criterion of nationhood today. Leaving aside the assumption that modernity and the present provide the models of nationhood to which all others must conform, we should note that in the second millennium BC Egypt was actually tied into a Near Eastern regional 'system' of states, along with the Hittite empire, the kingdom of Mitanni and the Kassites of Babylon. It is, in fact, a period about which we have some knowledge because of the diplomatic correspondence that has survived, the Tell-el-Amarna letters. But, whether these polities can be characterized as 'nations' because of their geopolitical interrelations, is quite another matter (Roux 1964).

In a much later, Hellenistic age, too, Egypt under the Ptolemies formed part of a regional 'international system' in the Near East which included Seleucid Syria, Pergamon, Macedon and Parthia. Here, too, states were formed that centred on distinctive territories with frontiers, with each community possessing its own cult, language, calendar, laws and customs (though the Seleucid empire in fact included several such communities). Perhaps, then, we should designate these political communities 'nations', and concur with the judgement of Doron Mendels that 'the nations of the ancient Near East that were the neighbours of the Jews had specific and well-defined symbols of political nationalism, namely, the temple, territory, kingship and the army' (1992: 1).

Even if the nationalism of the ancient world bears a different sense from that of 'modern times', and the issue in Hellenistic times was, in Mendels' words, one 'of ethnicity, which will for convenience here be called "nationalism"', must we not concede the ubiquitous presence of nations in antiquity that resemble, in all their main features, those of modernity? Should we not, therefore, accept the perennial recurrence of nations in successive epochs?[22]

This is a point taken up by Steven Grosby in his perceptive analysis of ancient Israel. Comparing the ancient Jews from the seventh century BC with other communities such as the ancient Greeks, Arameans, Edomites, Egyptians and Armenians, Grosby takes their collective self-image as nations seriously and underlines the primordial character of the relationship of a people to its land: in his formulation, 'a people has its land and a land has its people'. By that date, the elites of the kingdom of Judah, at least, possessed firm beliefs in the existence of a Jewish 'people' living in its own trans-local, bounded sacred territory and worshipping a single god, Yahweh, in a prescribed centre, the Temple in Jerusalem (Grosby 1991: 240).

In much the same manner, ancient Egyptians displayed a similar attachment to 'the land' (of the Nile), holding fast to the belief that Egypt belonged exclusively to the Egyptians and was under the protection and jurisdiction of the supreme god of the land – Amon-Re of Thebes – a belief that, according to Grosby, was lacking in ancient Greece, but could be found in ancient Armenia (ibid.: 247; 1997: 21).[23]

Nevertheless, such interpretations are subject to many qualifications. The paucity of evidence from the ancient world, and the dangers of a 'retrospective nationalism', of reading earlier epochs in the light of later concepts and preoccupations, make such an analysis at best tentative. Grosby himself is aware of the problems of evidence and category analysis: 'Rarely does a collectivity correspond with exactitude to a particular analytic category. This is true not only for the collectivities of antiquity, but for the modern national state as well' (Grosby 1997: 2).

There is a further, related problem. Even if we could legitimately speak of 'nations' in antiquity, that does not entail any continuity with particular modern nations. An ancient Egyptian or Greek nation may bear little relationship to a modern Egyptian or Greek nation, despite territorial and, in the Greek case, linguistic continuities. That is the burden of Paschalis Kitromilides' incisive modernist critiques of Greek nationalist historiography and Greek nationalism. It was, he says, the great *History of the Greek Nation* by Konstantinos Paparrigopoulos in the mid-nineteenth century that first presented the idea of a continuous Greek nation as a collective actor, persisting continuously from classical antiquity through the splendour of a Greek Byzantium to the modern independent Greek state. Whereas, in point of fact, according to Kitromilides, during the medieval epoch right up to the early nineteenth century, Greece and Greeks became one part of the far-flung Byzantine empire and Orthodox ecumene (and later, the Ottoman empire), as had the other modern and newly imagined political communities of Serbia, Bulgaria and Rumania (Kitromilides 1989 and 1998; see also Just 1989).

Were the Greek nationalists, then, entirely wrong when they posited a Greek nation peristing from the Byzantine empire, if not from classical Greece, and, per contra, are the modernists justified in claiming that a Greek nation only emerged in the early nineteenth century, with the advent of modernity? Insofar as the modernists define the nation in terms of mass citizenship, public culture and bordered territory, there can be no doubt that a Greek nation was inconceivable before the modern epoch. But, if we press these criteria, can we really speak of a Greek nation before the Greek defeat of 1922 by the Turks and the subsequent exchange of populations and stabilization of its borders? The modernists also face the problem of 'mass participation' in the (Greek) nation and, on that score, we can hardly speak of a Greek 'nation' before the twentieth century. If, on the other hand, we define the nation, with the neo-perennialists, in terms of ethnicity, vernacular language and religious culture, a Greek nation might be said to exist in the later Byzantine empire, as well as in the subsequent Orthodox millet which was led by Greeks and a Greek-speaking clergy. Moreover, though demographic continuity was largely broken during the invasions of Greece by the Avars, Slavs and Albanians from the sixth century, a case can even be made for a tenuous *cultural* link with classical Greece following the revival of Greek philosophy and language in the later Byzantine empire (Baynes and Moss 1969: ch. 1; Armstrong 1982: 174–81).

Similar problems of historical interpretation can be found in other modern nations with a claim to a continuous past stretching back to antiquity. Egyptians, Persians, Armenians and Jews all suffered massive demographic and cultural caesuras, either within the land of their early development and independence, or through expulsion and migration from the 'homeland'. In the case of the Egyptians and Persians, to religious conversion there was added a large influx of cultural aliens – Greeks, Arameans, Arabs and Turks. At different points in time, alien ethnic groups occupied the country and established their dynasties – in the Egyptian case until the twentieth century, and in Persia until the Constitutional movement of the early twentieth century. In the case of the Armenians and Jews, to successive foreign occupations – Babylonian, Persian, Hellenistic, Roman and Byzantine – were added emigration and expulsion, and the consequent pre-eminence of a diaspora community, which never severed its links with the historic homeland. But, can we term a diaspora community a 'nation'? Or can we only speak of an Armenian and Jewish nation in the twentieth century, following the creation of more or less independent states in parts of their historic territories, with the possibility of permanent borders, a public culture and mass participation?[24]

Nations in History: An Alternative View

But do we have to accept either of these interpretations? The evidence, on either definition, is at best unclear. Take the question of borders. Giddens, for example, puts forward a modernist argument that premodern polities had fluctuating and indeterminate frontiers, while modern polities are characterized by more or less permanent and fixed borders. There is much to be said for this contrast, but it is not as absolute as he claims. Ancient empires had very clear ideas about their territorial limits; the northern frontier of the Roman empire, for example, hardened for over a century into a fixed border, just as the Chinese sought to fix their northern frontier with the Great Wall. The ancient Egyptians were blessed with clear and fixed eastern, western and northern borders – as were the Japanese, once they had conquered the Ainu. As for the Jews, the Bible set out, if somewhat uncertainly, the borders of the promised land.

The same goes for the criteria of mass 'public culture' and 'citizenship'. Measured by twentieth-century standards, most premodern communities were lacking in both respects. For one thing, most of them had ethno-religious definitions of membership and culture; for another, as we saw, there are few records of how far premodern populations were involved in the elite culture of their communities. On the other hand, there are hints of such involvement in the ancient world, through the great religious festivals, temple worship, legal regulations, markets and trade fairs, as well as conscription for war; and, in the medieval epoch, under the aegis of the great world religions, such involvement became more regular and direct, though rarely political.

All this suggests that the modernists are right to insist on the importance of the differences between the type of nation found in the modern world and earlier collective cultural identities. At the same time, we should be careful not to create too great a disjunction between these 'premodern communities' and 'modern nations', nor to disallow in advance, as Hobsbawm does, any kind of continuity between premodern communities and modern nations. Such a gulf exists only when we confine our attention to the upper strata who, from being generally cosmopolitan and cross-cultural in premodern epochs, become increasingly national, and nationalist, in the modern epoch. Such a gulf also exists when we contrast the modern epoch with a single 'premodern' age, treated almost monolithically, thereby creating an artificial 'before-and-after' model of events. By taking our historical enquiry back to early antiquity, we can discern different patterns and stages of collective cultural identities, and hopefully provide a more nuanced and complex account of their development (see McNeill 1986; cf. A. D. Smith 1994).

Ethnic categories and ethnies

The first such pattern, and probably the earliest stage in recorded history, is that of *'ethnic categories'* – populations who possess a collective proper name and share one or more cultural attributes, usually language and customs, which differentiate them from others, and who usually have, or are thought to have, some link with a particular territory, though this may be shifting and uncertain. Such categories are seen from the outside as 'ethnic', that is, as having a common origin and history, even if the population itself has no myth of common ancestry. Such categories are, as Hastings says, fluid and often transient, because they have no fixed boundaries, and no symbols or myths, encoded in texts and artefacts. A common ethnicity is attributed to the population by outsiders, but not felt within, or at least, we have no record or means of knowing whether the members possess any collective ties and sentiments.

This situation, and description, begins to change with the appearance of genealogies. Families combine in a village or neighbourhood through intermarriage, and begin to trace their lines of descent to common ancestors. Such genealogies are usually handed down orally, but later may be committed to writing in chronicles and epic poems. These kinship myths of ethnic origins and descent are often linked to migration memories and to rituals, symbols and myths of a common cult, which link the human to the cosmic world, and place the union of families under divine protection. The more closely the genealogical myths and migration memories are interwoven with the cult and its rituals, the stronger become the ties and sentiments of the members, turning them first into a dense ethnic network of shared activities and relations, and then into a fully fledged 'ethnic community' or *ethnie* – a named human population with myths of shared origins, common historical memories, one or more elements of common culture, a link with a homeland and a strong sentiment of solidarity, at least among the elites. Such communities usually possess a variety of economic, social and political institutions, durable and visible boundaries and a well-defined sense of outsiders or strangers, frequently reinforced by regular cross-border activity, such as trade, mobility and exchange of ideas and techniques (see Barth 1969: Introduction; Nash 1989; Eriksen 1993).

In the early epochs, then, two or three patterns emerge – of ethnic categories, networks and communities; and there is frequent moving back and forth of populations between these different kinds of ethnic formation. Such a stage is not, of course, confined to early antiquity and the first recorded histories. We continue to find a variety of ethnic groupings – categories, networks and communities – right into the modern epoch, not only in Africa and Asia, but among some European populations as well. This tells us that the patterns of collective cultural identities outlined here do not form an evolutionary series. The patterns exhibit considerable fluidity and overlap, and there is nothing determinate, let alone irreversible, about their historical sequence.

Ethnic states and early nations

The ancient world is, in large part, one of ethnic groupings, as well as city-states, kingdoms and empires. Many of the looser ethnic groupings do not take political forms or reveal political aspirations. On the other hand, those that have crystallized as full ethnic communities tend to seek political expression and form what we may term 'ethnic states'. This is particularly the case where a powerful priesthood seeks a monopoly of cultural expression and allies itself with the ruling elite to produce a fairly cohesive and unitary ethnic kingdom. This was the case in ancient Egypt and, to some extent, in the much more ethnically heterogenous Achaemenid and, later, Sassanid Iran. There was little of that horizontal cross-class sentiment binding the population which we find in nations, since the nobility and clergy received a different kind of education, though in ancient Egypt, the culture of the upper classes filtered downwards, aided by the unique geography and geopolitics of the Nile valley, and the priestly near-monopoly of culture (see Frye 1966; David 1982).

The situation was rather different in ancient Israel and Armenia (there is too little evidence to make a secure judgement about the Arameans). The rise of powerful myths and symbols, memories and traditions of community, migration, territory and history, imbued the Armenians and Jews with not only a sense of difference from outsiders, but also of fraternity, if not sorority, within. Here, monotheistic religion undoubtedly played a powerful formative role. Though class differences continued to be prominent, especially in Armenia with its landowning nobility, a sense of communal fate and political solidarity can be found at all levels of society. This is most obvious in the case of the ancient Jewish prophets and the response to their calls for repentance and return to the Torah, but we also find a sense of common fate among Armenian elites, after the destruction of the Armenian kingdom, in the writings of the historians of early Christian Armenia, notably Moses of Khorene. In both cases, the sense of difference and commonality is combined with a desire for political autonomy which, despite being ultimately disappointed, points back towards an ideal or 'golden age' of independence, and fuels the hope of future political restoration (see Lang 1980; Zeitlin 1984; Grosby 1997; Panossian 2000).

In these cases, it makes sense to speak of 'nations' in the ancient world, albeit cautiously and on a limited scale, marking the onset of a new pattern alongside that of the more

common ethnic states. True, we cannot claim mass participation in politics (or only for adult males in classical Athens),
let alone full legal citizenship or economic unity. But, as we
have seen, a strict application of these criteria would rule out
many so-called modern nations and delay the timing of the
emergence of most 'nations', even in democracies, until after
World War I.

This, perhaps, is the nub of the matter. For most modernists, nations can really only be found in democratic societies, for only in such societies can we truly speak of mass
citizenship. Once again, the Eurocentric and Western assumptions of this evolutionary scheme of national development
come into view. And, once again, this is to impose modern
contexts and criteria onto epochs that had quite different concerns and assumptions. What mattered for most people in the
ancient world was how they stood in relation to the forces
of an often inexplicable and violent nature controlled by the
gods who had to be propitiated through collective rites and
sacrifices. In these circumstances, the horizontal fraternity of
citizenship in the modern world finds its counterpart in
popular participation in large-scale cults and rituals, in the
performance of ethical and religious obligations which bind
a community of presumed ancestry into a community of faith
and worship, in the sense of community evoked by symbols
and myths of ethnic origins and election, and in shared memories of ancestors and heroic deeds. Where such a fusion has
occurred, we may begin to speak of nationhood, with religious law and ritual playing the equivalent role of the legal
rights and duties of modern citizenship. In this way, we might
speak of distinctive ancient forms of the nation.[25]

Dynastic and patrician nations

A third pattern is the one charted by Adrian Hastings: that
of the medieval dynastic and/or patrician nations of Europe.
On the one hand, there are the strong dynastic nations of the
West, based on 'lateral' *ethnies* and strong states – in
England, Scotland, France, Denmark, Sweden and Spain –
emerging from the twelfth to the fifteenth century; and
finding an echo in a few East European states, notably

Poland, Russia and, for a period, Hungary. On the other
hand, a more patrician and middle-class, and less unified,
kind of nation emerges, yet with a strong sense of ethnic difference, feelings of religious fraternity and a desire for political autonomy, all of which were linked to specific ancestral
homelands and a common culture, religious or linguistic, or
both. I have in mind late medieval Switzerland and the
Netherlands, and also, to a lesser extent, medieval Ireland,
despite its chronic political divisions. In these cases, powerful myths, symbols and memories of heroic deeds inspired a
more exclusive and faith-oriented, though less united, kind
of community (see de Paor 1986; Schama 1987; Im Hof
1991).

The differences between these two kinds of late medieval
nation, dynastic and patrician, should not be exaggerated.
Both are products, in varying degrees, of 'lateral' aristocratic
ethnies, the culture of whose ruling classes was filtered down
to the middle classes and some outlying regions. In the dynastic nation, the agent of such cultural dissemination was the
strong ethnic state, whose rulers sought to weld together and
unify, by a process of 'bureaucratic incorporation', different
classes and regions into a compact national state. In the patrician nation, a more or less compact aristocracy or urban
patriciate had been created through conflicts with outside
powers (as well among themselves), supported by spiritual
leaders in periods of often intense religious fervour. The
ensuing geopolitical separation, and even a degree of isolation, encouraged the spread of this religious culture to the
middle and lower strata. Such slow, and often uneven
processes of medieval national formation need to be distinguished in turn from the more telescoped and purposive
processes of middle-class nation-creation by intelligentsias
and bourgeoisies in the modern period (see A. D. Smith
1989).

It is important to remember that, in the world at large
throughout this period, ethnic groupings of various kinds pre-
dominated. Nations, whether dynastic or more patrician and
upper middle class, remained the exception, even after the
Renaissance and Reformation. The Swiss, Dutch and Irish
examples were not replicated across Europe, let alone the
world, until the advent of revolutionary nationalism. Nor, for

that matter, were the Western and Northern European dynastic national states, except in Poland, Russia and, for a time, Hungary. The Far Eastern 'ethnic states' of China, Korea and Japan, as well as Thailand, Cambodia and Vietnam and, further west, Sassanid Persia (many of them, in fact, containing small or large minorities) revealed little feeling of fraternity and insufficient sustained unity to match their sense of ethnic difference vis-à-vis outsiders and their desire to retain political autonomy in their ancestral homelands. Class differences were marked, and there was little in the way of mass participation in cultic worship, except perhaps in Japan, and little economic unity or legal standardization across the whole population and territory.

Until the Tokugawa Shogunate (1603–1868) in Japan, that is. From the seventeenth century onwards, and the enforced isolation of Japan from the outside world, a growing middle-class culture and solidarity, supported by Japan's relative ethnic homogeneity and island geography, helped to carry a sense of chosenness and fuelled historical and cultural revivals that presaged the later restoration of the Emperor under the Meiji regime. If the Meiji leaders hoped to make the past serve the present, they also sought to place the present under the sign of a favourable and glorious past; and, while the Western invasion provided the initial stimulus for change, the form and content of that change were the products of internal developments within Tokugawa Japan and, further back, the chronicled legacies of an imperial past. Here, then, an ethnically relatively homogenous, middle-class nation formed the basis for modern Japanese nationalism after 1868 (see Lehmann 1982; but cf. Doak 1997).

The other possible exception was Safavid Persia (1501–1722). Before that time, successive dynasties, often ruling parts of the Iranian plateau, reinforced Iran's ethnic and geographical diversity and impeded the growth of any cross-class fraternity and participation. A sense of distinctive Persian identity and chosenness which had flowered in the New Persian linguistic revival of the tenth and eleventh centuries remained confined to small literate elites in the succeeding centuries. However, after 1501 a powerful dynasty of Turkic origins instituted a political revival and a cultural renaissance that was fuelled by their militant Shi'ite faith.

Conversely, their unification of Iran helped to spread Twelver Shi'ism from Shah Abbas' capital, Isfahan, throughout Iran, with the result that by 1722 most Persian speakers had become Shi'ite, and Persian identity became increasingly, if unintentionally, coextensive with Shi'ism. Even if this revival waned under the succeeding Afghan Qajjar dynasty (1796–1925), it laid the foundations of a distinctive middle-class ethnic Persian sense of solidarity which found political expression in the 1905–6 constitutional movement (see Cottam 1979; Keddie 1981: chs 1–3).

Revolutionary nationalist nations

Middle-class nationalism   Beginning with the Dutch revolt and the English Civil War, a new and much more cohesive and purposive kind of nation was born. It was, at first, fuelled by a militant, reformed and puritanical version of Christianity, with a heightened sense of ethnic chosenness, which not only threw up a new type of regime – puritan Islamic movements had done as much through the centuries – but a new kind of demand for political autonomy and popular participation, based on Old Testament models. The key concepts which summed up these demands were those of 'nation' and 'citizen'. Together, they pointed the way towards a bourgeois democratic nationalism, in which a culturally distinctive 'people' would become the sole legitimate source of power, and membership of that people the only means of acquiring the freedoms and rights that accrued to citizens. This middle-class national-democratic logic was developed by the *philosophes* and publicists of the French Enlightenment, to the point where it undermined the assumptions, and broke the bonds, of the absolutist state and its system of privileged orders, based largely upon birth (see Walzer 1985).

But the nationalist element of this development proved every bit as vital as the democratic. For the appeal to the 'nation', which stemmed in France in the first place from the defence of their liberties by the *parlements* in their battles with a centralizing absolutism, harked back to earlier concepts of 'national character' and the 'genius of the nation', which had been developed by the landed gentry and upper middle classes first in England and then in France at the turn of the eighteenth century. These ideas, in turn, drew upon, and secularized, still older ethnic memories and religious beliefs in ethnic election – the conviction that God protected and blessed those peoples who obeyed His commandments and faithfully fulfilled the mission with which they had been entrusted. In France, such a belief, linked to the prototype of ancient Israel and centred on the figure of the king and his realm, can be traced back to at least the thirteenth century, and early formulations can be found as far back as the kingdom of the Franks, as they can among the Anglo-Saxons (see Armstrong 1982: 154–9; Beaune 1985).

It was among 'vertical' or demotic *ethnies*, and a secular-izing intelligentsia, that such ideas found particular reso-nance. In Central and Eastern Europe, and then in Asia and Africa in the early twentieth century, intellectuals and pro-fessionals sought to return to their ethnic heritage and ver-nacular cultures, and to mobilize the middle, and on occasion the lower, classes for political action. 'Vernacular mobiliza-tion' on behalf of demotic *ethnies* involved the rediscovery, appropriation and politicization of an indigenous culture by a returning intelligentsia, as the basis for popular agitation and political claims. Such a 'bottom-up' approach was par-ticularly attractive to those whose communities had been long incorporated in, and subjected to, large and often oppressive empires, and who lacked powerful institutions which could 'carry' and impose the new vision and its political aims (see A. D. Smith 1986: ch. 4, and 1989).

So, it was not long before other peoples outside Western Europe, led by their intelligenstias, sought and found a sense of nationhood based upon the conviction of the cultural uniqueness and, ultimately, ethnic election of their demotic *ethnies*. What was new, from the late eighteenth century, was the provision of a ready-made blueprint for translating that conviction into a political programme of national autonomy, unity and identity. National*ism*, the political ideology, was born of this fusion of a pre-existing sense of ethnic ancestry and election with the revolutionary ideals of popular partici-pation and autonomy pioneered by the intellectuals and middle classes. From this union was born the doctrine of national self-determination and its progeny of different kinds of national identity, based on criteria as diverse as language, ethnicity, territory, religion, history and pigmentation – criteria that gave rise to several kinds of nationalism, not just a duality of territorial-political and ethno-linguistic nationalisms (See Armstrong 1995).

Mass nationalisms   The success of the middle-class Anglo-French national model had profound social and geopolitical implications, both within Europe and outside. First, it became possible for others to analyse the components of that success, ideological as well as economic and political. This meant that a 'blueprint' of the form and content of that success could be extracted, which entailed a national format, based on:

(1)   an historic territory or homeland, preferably one that was relatively compact;
(2)   a territorially unified, and socially cohesive, if not homogeneous, population;
(3)   a unified economy with a single occupational system and mobility throughout the territory;
(4)   a single, shared and distinctive public culture, with preferably a single language;
(5)   a set of distinctive myths and collective memories, with preferably a unified history; and
(6)   common rights and duties for all members, together with participation as citizens in a largely autonomous, and preferably independent and sovereign, national community.

Given the variety of criteria of a national identity, it was hardly surprising to find a series of attempts by a host of self-defined 'peoples' to use the nationalist blueprint in different ways to realize their aspirations for greater autonomy, unity and identity. Following the United Irishmen's uprising of 1798, the early nineteenth century saw a growing national resistance to Napoleon's imperial-national ambitions in Spain, Russia and Germany, with Serbia and Greece subsequently staging revolts against the Ottoman empire, soon to be followed by a failed Polish revolt against the Tsarist empire and a successful bid to create a separate Belgian state. Moreover, from 1810 onwards, the creole elites of Spain's Latin American provinces succeeded in dissolving her empire and founding a series of Latin American states. While it is arguable how far these revolts possessed a specifically nationalist dimension at the time, they undoubtedly acquired an increasingly fervent nationalism from the 1820s on, demonstrating once again the logic of national-democratic development and the power and utility of the nationalist blueprint (see Humphreys and Lynch 1965; Anderson 1991: ch. 4).

As the nineteenth century progressed, not only did the number of such self-defined nations increase across Europe, and subsequently Asia, but the democratic logic of the nationalist blueprint soon found its full expression in the extension of the franchise and the inclusion of all members as legally equal citizens of the national community, though not without struggles, setbacks and interruptions. By the early twentieth century, this had come to include women, and in the course of the later twentieth century, young adults of both sexes. Democratic mass nationalism, with an increasingly socioeconomic content, which was in the main a product of the world wars and modern technology, appears as a revolutionary development. Yet it was not wholly unprecedented. Not only was it a logical development of the earlier middle-class nationalist blueprint; its origins can be traced back to some of the early and medieval nations' sense of chosenness and mission. The elevation of 'the people' and its social and cultural needs, characteristic of modern mass ethnic nationalism, harks back to the sense of the community of the faithful found in early ethnic communities and nations in the ancient and medieval worlds, some of which have served as prototypes for later nations. By the mid-twentieth century, such latterday 'chosen peoples' and their mass nationalisms were expressing, and testing in war, their rediscovered identities in myths, symbols, values and memories of conflict, conquest and resistance, and in the expulsion and extermination of whole peoples (see Carr 1945; Marwick 1974; A. D. Smith 1981b).

Conclusion

It is not necessary to recount the story of the diffusion of revolutionary nationalism and its role in the creation of mass nations, from the 1848 revolutions through the epoch of racial nationalisms, to the anti-colonial nationalisms after 1945 and the latest efflorescence of ethnic nationalisms. However, three aspects of these movements need to be highlighted.

The first is their *ideological* novelty. These are ideology-based movements and, as a result, usually ideologically based nations. They depend upon a near-universal acceptance of the legitimacy of national*ism*, and are judged, and judge themselves, according to its tenets. That is, they measure themselves, and are evaluated, according to the components of the nationalist blueprint. Their renewal nationalisms, too, are attempts to approximate more closely to the blueprint, after a period of relative stagnation or movement away ('decline') from it. This, I think, makes the modern nationalist-based nations different from the earlier pre-nationalist nations in the medieval period or antiquity. The latter nations did not possess an ideological blueprint or standard; their nationalisms were purely particularistic, embedded in the historical circumstances in which the premodern nation found itself. They possessed no 'theory' of nations, only a set of goals and sentiments peculiar to the particular nation. Hence, their nationalisms could not be replicated or spread; there was no system of general ideas to hand which could be applied universally and produce certain kinds of action towards common goals. In that sense, national*ism*, the ideology, has proved to be a watershed in the development of human association and communication.

The second aspect is the importance of an *ethnic basis* for modern nations. This we have already seen, not only among the early nations, but in the case of the popular nationalisms of the twentieth century. They too have drawn on antecedent ethnic ties and sentiments, defining the 'national self' according to different criteria, but always seeking the greatest continuity with the cultural past of the dominant *ethnie*. It is easy to dismiss such efforts as no more than nationalist fabrications and mythical inventions. Some nationalist intellectuals no doubt deluded themselves, or even cynically manipulated mass sentiments, as Kedourie claimed. But their frequent success suggests a different interpretation, one that emphasizes the need for popular 'resonance' and 'appeal'. Since, on the whole, large numbers of people will not respond over the long term to pure inventions – as the fate of Esperanto suggests – the rediscoveries and reconstructions of the intellectuals and others had to remain as close to popular perceptions as possible. They had to adhere to the cultural parameters of the 'traditions of the people', politicizing their sense of ethnic community, and reinterpreting those traditions as deep cultural resources for a political struggle for national self-determination.

The final point concerns the *inner world* of *ethnies* and nations. The appeal to 'the people' can only be conducted through the discovery and use of their collective memories, symbols, myths, values and traditions. Similarly, our analysis, if it is to penetrate this inner realm, must seek out and analyse these ethno-symbolic elements. The shared memories of golden ages, ancestors and great heroes and heroines, the communal values that they embody, the myths of ethnic origins, migration and divine election, the symbols of community, territory, history and destiny that distinguish them, as well as their various traditions and customs of kinship and sacrifice, provide the keys to understanding the relationship of the ethnic past to the national present and future, and in particular the links, and ruptures, between ethnic communities and nations, premodern and modern. No analysis that ignores these ethno-symbolic components will enable us to grasp the present self-understandings of nations, or their peculiar beliefs about their own histories and destinies. And, without an adequate grasp of the inner history of nations, we shall find ourselves unable to gauge their future development in a global era.

6
Prospects

Appearances to the contrary, the holocausts of the world wars did nothing to abate the power and ubiquity of popular social nationalisms. On the contrary, if anything, they received a new impetus and power from the involvement of civilians in total warfare. Despite the almost frozen silence surrounding the subject of nationalism, at least in the West and the communist states, broken only by the surge of hope that accompanied the movements of decolonization in Africa and Asia, the nations of Europe and America were more than ever firmly rooted in the political landscape. Even though the United Nations consisted only of states and the principle of self-determination enshrined in the UN Charter applied only to liberated colonies, the legitimacy accorded to popular consent, and the near-universal acceptance of 'nationalist' propositions as the sole grounds for the exercise of state power revealed the extent to which the nation had become entrenched as the cornerstone of a society of states in the second half of the twentieth century.

Proliferating Nationalism

Subsequent developments did little to undermine the centrality of the nation and the nationalist principle. The earliest of these, the process of decolonization, was carried out in the name of the self-same principle of national legitimacy and popular sovereignty which obtained in Europe and the Americas, with the rider that, in these cases, the principle was only being used to create new nations out of recently acquired colonies, albeit on the foundations of older societies and cultures. This was the era of 'nation-building', in which societies in Africa and Asia were, for the most part, being refashioned by entirely new states after the European model.[1]

Hard on its heels came the so-called 'ethnic revival' in the industrialized societies of the West – in Quebec and Flanders, Scotland and Catalonia, Brittany and Euzkadi, Corsica and Wales. Here, a largely middle-class revolt of 'peripheral minorities' against the dominant ethnic majorities of old-established states and against their centralized governments appealed to some of the older symbols, myths and memories of classic European mass nationalisms, though with a more social and often socialist programme and more limited political goals – in most cases a desire for cultural and economic autonomy, rather than outright independence. In the late 1960s and 1970s, following on from the civil rights movement in America, these ethnic autonomy movements overlapped with student, feminist and ecology movements to create considerable tensions in the established democratic states, forcing a reappraisal, still under way, of their functions and viability in a world of resurgent ethno-regional loyalties.[2]

The repercussions of this challenge in the West had hardly abated when the new policies of *perestroika* and *glasnost* in the former Soviet Union brought into the open the national cleavages and ethnic aspirations in Eastern Europe and the Soviet republics. Starting even earlier in Poland, the tensions and conflicts, apparent from the mid-1980s in the Baltic states, the Ukraine, the Caucasus and Central Asia, helped to speed, even if they did not cause, the break-up of the Soviet Union and its empire along ethno-national lines. One consequence of this new wave of ethnic nationalisms was to restore a measure of popular legitimacy to the aspirations of smaller peoples and subordinate nations, and more generally to nationalism, insofar as these popular movements appeared at the time to be motivated by a genuine desire for collective

freedom and democracy. Even if subsequent events in Eastern
Europe, the former Soviet Union and, especially, the Balkans,
did not always bear out such hopes, and instead seemed to
confirm an inextricable bond between an exclusive ethnic
nationalism and neo-fascism, racism and 'ethnic cleansing',
the map of Europe had once more been largely recast along
the lines of existing ethno-national cleavages, while East
European politics had become increasingly bound up with the
needs and interests of nationally defined states and their
elites.[3]

If we add to these developments the continuing proliferation of ethnic nationalisms, as well as the persistence of territorial nationalisms, in the new states of Africa and Asia –
from the Tamils and Moro, to the Kurds, Southern Sudanese
and Eritreans – we may wonder that any observer could still
seriously suggest the waning of nationalism, let alone its
imminent demise.

Yet that is exactly the claim of Eric Hobsbawm, and it is
one made in full cognizance of the current proliferation of
ethnic and territorial nationalisms. What can Hobsbawm,
and those who think like him, have in mind?

For Hobsbawm, the current spate of nationalisms is temporary; it masks the real 'movement of history' which is
towards ever larger units of human association. Nationalism
will continue to exist, but only in a minor and secondary role.
What Hobsbawm does not tell us is whether *nations* will
cease to be important. For, even if 'nation-states' have lost
their former economic and military functions, as Hobsbawm
claims, does this entail the withering away of 'nations'? Does
loss of state sovereignty imply a diminution of national identity? (Hobsbawm 1990: ch. 6).

Such questions point to the complexity of issues surrounding the so-called 'supersession' or 'transcendence' of
nations and nationalism. We are, in fact, faced with at least
three different claims and the ensuing debates. The first concerns the 'nation-state' and its imminent demise or persistence, the second focuses on the transformations and possible
fragmentation of 'national identity', while the third concen-
trates on the decline and possible supersession of ideologies
of 'nationalism'. I shall take these in turn.

The Demise of the Nation-state?

The claim that a certain kind of political community, often called the 'nation-state', is in terminal decline is usually made on economic and political grounds. It assumes that:

(1) the term 'nation-state' signifies a clear and distinct type of political community, which we can isolate;
(2) we can then measure deviations from this type over time, and demonstrate a decline in its power and/or cohesion since the Second World War;
(3) such a trajectory is determined by historical changes and socio-political transformations which will leave no room for 'nation-states', except in a folkloristic manner.

1.   As we have seen, there are very few pure instances of the type of political community called the 'nation-state'. A nation-state can be said to exist only where more or less the whole population of a state belongs to a single ethno-national group and where the boundaries of the group and those of the state are co-extensive. Only then do 'nation' and 'state' coincide. But such coincidence is extremely rare, particularly in today's world of migration and cultural mingling. Instead, we have the much more common type of political community known as the 'national state', that is, a state where the great majority of the population belong to a single or dominant ethno-national group, even though other small ethnic groups are found within the state's borders, and where the political community is legitimated in terms of the tenets of nationalist ideology (see Connor 1972; Wiberg 1983).

2.   Even if we could show the wide applicability of the concept of the 'nation-state', it would be difficult to demonstrate a definite trend towards decline in its power and/or cohesion; and there is even less chance of doing so in the case of national states. The argument assumes that, at some point in the nineteenth century, the national (or nation-) state was the dominant form of political organization, and that it declined from that plateau of power and cohesion as a result of the loss of its major functions, especially after the Second World War. The main index of power and cohesion is usually

taken to be complete sovereignty or, at least, a high degree of autonomy in the conduct of external affairs. In fact, few national states in the last two centuries have exercised untrammelled sovereignty; states were bound by various treaties and understandings, and their capacities for effecting changes in general were limited by the relatively undeveloped technologies and communications at their disposal. This is as true of the external sphere of foreign affairs and warfare, as it is of domestic control and infrastructural change. True, state capacities greatly increased in the late nineteenth century and thereafter, but they bore no comparison with contemporary state powers, and they were confined to a handful of great powers. The same is true of state cohesion. While the challenge of contemporary ethnic and regional movements should not be underestimated, most national states throughout the last two centuries have seen ethnic, religious and regional challenges, albeit on a lesser scale. The chances of securing political solidarity are also much greater today, insofar as mass communications, propaganda techniques and public education allow state elites to instil in their populations common values, sentiments and beliefs, especially if these are 'national' in character. This is certainly one reason for the persistence of territorial and ethnic nationalisms (see Kahan 1968).

3.   It is quite true that the national state has lost many of its former economic functions, and that it has seen its military freedom severely curtailed since the introduction of nuclear, chemical and biological weapons. The rise of huge currency and trading markets and vast transnational companies with budgets, personnel, investment and technical expertise that far outstrip those of many smaller states, and the creation of huge political and military blocs and multinational command structures, have undoubtedly eroded the economic autonomy and limited the military options of even the most powerful states. But, the degree of such erosion is difficult to measure, given the limitations on the exercise of economic and military power by national states in earlier periods. In any case, it is amply compensated by the acquisition of new functions by the national state in the name of its national character and the welfare of its citizenry. What we have been witnessing is a shift of state functions and powers

from the economic and military to the social and cultural spheres, and from external sovereignty to internal, domestic control. One has only to think of the vast increase in state regulation of areas such as mass, public education, health and genetics, population and environmental planning, immigration, the mass media, the arts, sport and culture, the professions and employment, the trade unions and wages, taxation and fiscal policy, and much more, to realize that, far from being in danger of decline, the national state is becoming much more centralized, coordinated and powerful. Besides, the state's primary function, law and order, while always influenced by external pressures, remains largely intact, and has become, and is perceived to be, the chief locus of state power and control. All in all, through its monitoring, regulatory and bureaucratic controls, the national state is able to intervene far more directly, persistently and comprehensively than at any time in modern, (let alone premodern) history.[4]

But this is only one side of the picture. The argument in favour of the decline of the national state also proceeds deductively, from the necessary effects of globalization. This is not the place to enter the vexed discussion on the various meanings of this concept. Suffice it to say that, in addition to economic interdependence and large-scale population movement, we are witnessing a high degree of time-and-space compression, in which events in one part of the world have immediate effects in other parts, as a result of the rapid growth of global mass communications, information technology and the like. But, whether this makes our globe all 'one place' is questionable. Even if national state boundaries have become more porous in recent decades, mass communications have not rendered borders obsolete or diminished the regulatory and supervisory controls of the national state. On the contrary, there is plenty of evidence that state elites have sought to increase their power over the flow of information and cultural products, often through multilateral agreements and treaties with other states. Again, the proliferation of inter-governmental and non-governmental organizations across the globe has curtailed some of the great powers' freedom of action (the many small powers never possessed much autonomy) through adherence to various conventions and treaties, but their overall effect has also been to increase the power and longevity of the national state, which is now assumed to be the only legitimate international actor.[5]

To this, it may be objected that the new economic and cultural forces have generated the need for much larger political units and cultural spaces, and that is why we are witnessing the growth of new continental associations and unions. The most notable of these is the European Union, which, from a limited customs union, has burgeoned into a much larger economic and political community bent on creating a genuine European federal state and European cultural identity. Despite the current European Union slogan of 'unity in diversity', there is little doubt that for pan-Europeans a real European unity and identity can only be achieved at the expense of national identity. At the very least, they would expect a considerable decrease in the power and intensity of national identities, and the transfer of existing loyalties to the national state upwards to the federal union – after the manner of the creation of the United States or Germany in the late eighteenth and nineteenth centuries. By securing a progressive transfer of functions and powers to the federal centre, they hope to create an institutional political framework which will, in the end, harness popular loyalties; in other words, they assume that identity change follows sovereignty transfer (see Wallace 1990; Riekmann 1997).

This assumed linkage between state sovereignty and national identity underlies much of the current debates between Europhiles and Eurosceptics, as well as the few referenda to date on the progress of the stages of European integration. It certainly permeates the opposition to entry into the Euro-currency in Denmark, Britain and possibly Sweden, as well as the Norwegian and Swiss refusal to enter the European Union. But are sovereignty and identity so closely interconnected? Rousseau's counsel to the Poles who had recently lost their independence to preserve their customs and culture, and the subsequent signal failure of attempts to diminish, let alone eradicate, a Polish national identity for over one hundred years, would suggest otherwise. In the European case, nothing like such state dismemberment is contemplated. On the contrary, European directives are meant to proceed through the national state and its institutions, once again endowing them with an added legitimacy and authority. Moreover, through the notion of 'subsidiarity', certain freedoms and powers are left to the states; what is demanded, instead, is a growing harmonization of state laws and actions in, first, the economic and social, and, thereafter, the political and military spheres, through a process of 'union from above'. The real issue, of course, is how far popular support in the constituent national states is likely to continue to underpin this project, and whether a European federal state is likely to supplant the existing national states in their major functions and powers, as well as in the political sentiments of their citizens.[6]

Hybrid Identities?

If the national state is challenged from above by larger political groups and associations, its national identity or inner bond of political solidarity is threatened from below by the claims of smaller cultural groups. In the last few decades, the world has experienced massive population movements that have begun to change the cultural composition and self-images of many societies, especially in the West. The recent influx of refugees and asylum-seekers, *Gastarbeiter* and ex-colonials has undermined the traditional values and beliefs of a single, homogeneous national identity, challenging the older national ideologies and pedagogical narratives of the unified nation and, in some versions, substituting a series of separate cultural communities loosely held together in an overarching 'national community'. In this 'multicultural nation', each self is defined in relationship to 'the other' and, in Homi Bhabha's view, the official texts give way to everyday, 'performative' narratives of the people in which perceptions of history and identity become split and doubled, the nation is fragmented into its constituent cultural parts and national identity becomes 'hybridized' (Bhabha 1990: ch. 16).[7]

There is little doubt that recent massive immigration has changed the cultural composition of many nations, in the same way that mass transportation and tourism, along with satellite communications and information technology, have raised popular awareness of other cultures and peoples to new levels, with the result that the old apparent certainties about the cultural unity of the nation and its single, if remote, ethnic origins, have been undermined. But, in reality, they were never certainties. There were always counter-myths of origin and alternative memories of national culture, even if some of them might become temporarily predominant – and official. This meant that 'national identity' was always being reinterpreted and refashioned by each generation. Romantic ethnic nationalists may have yearned for a homogeneous whole and a seamless nation, expressing a single authentic 'soul', but this represented a distant ideal and only rarely a political programme. Even when the national state sought to create a unified citizenry through mass public education, so it too responded to the changing beliefs and conceptions of the nature of the 'national identity', which it sought to forge and transmit to the young. After all, most modern states have been ethnically plural and heterogeneous, and most nationalists have sought national unity, and only rarely national homogeneity. National unity may not have been the mirage that William McNeill claims it was; it was usually interpreted loosely, as a collective achievement and commitment, as, in Renan's words, 'a large-scale solidarity, constituted by the feeling of the sacrifices one has made in the past and of those one is prepared to make in the future' (1882, cited in Bhabha 1990: 19; cf. McNeill 1986: ch. 2). Whether as a result of this cultural pluralism or of long-term historical reasons, many Western states have come to operate with a more civic and territorial version of nationalism, through which immigrants and refugees may find a legitimate place in the host nation as citizens. On occasion, they may be invited to join in the cultural work of reinterpreting the nation and its political identity, so as to include their cultures and outlooks as constituent elements of a new overall national identity.

Nevertheless, there are definite limits to the possibilities of national reinterpretation. A single public culture and a distinct set of common rights and duties need to be identified and legitimated, along with an historic homeland. Political solidarity requires that some myths of origin, historical memories and collective symbols be cultivated. Such myths, symbols and memories need to resonate among large sections of the population included in the designated nation or national state if people are to feel a sense of collective belonging and engage in common action. That may require something more than a purely civic and territorial nationalism in which residence and republican loyalty constitute the main criteria of citizenship of the nation. The latter may need to be combined with, or even replaced by, other cultural criteria of nationhood, perhaps including a genealogical test of national solidarity, in which only those born of parents of the dominant *ethnie* are deemed to be members of the nation and hence citizens of the national state. In this way, even in a rational and liberal state like France, we witnessed an originally more civic and territorial French nationalism manifest in the Revolution give way during the Dreyfus Affair and under the Vichy regime to a much narrower view of the French nation, as belonging exclusively to those born in France of French and Catholic descent, with the corollary that this cultural France must be purified of corroding alien elements, cultural and physical, which appear to threaten the nation's moral cohesion and cultural individuality (see Viroli 1995).[8]

If this is the case, we must treat with caution claims that national identities in the modern Western states have become 'hybridized' and fragmented, and that the basic segment of population has become the culture group of either native or immigrant provenance, as opposed to the higher-order and overarching nation. Modern nations may have more than one face, and intermarriage rates may be encouraging a more culturally mixed population than we have witnessed in the recent past, but many of the states in question retain their dominant *ethnies* of long standing, and, outside of the great cities, most members of the dominant *ethnie* maintain their indigenous, albeit changing, cultures, memories, symbols and myths of origin. The fact that ideas of national identity are constantly being debated and periodically revised in the West suggests that such collective cultural identities serve important purposes and meet vital needs in the modern epoch. National identities are, if anything, even more desired outside the West, where the need to locate peoples thrown together by colonialism, and to provide a measure of political security and cultural belonging, is even more pressing. Although, as Partha Chatterjee so vividly demonstrates, more than one such 'national identity' can be discerned in a large and variegated population, such as we find in the Indian sub-continent, attempts to create an overarching set of traditions, symbols, myths and memories for the political community of the nation are the necessary concomitant of contemporary political struggles and large-scale popular mobilization in the new states of Africa and Asia (Chatterjee 1993; see also Brown 1994).

The Dissolution of Nationalism?

If national identities retain their importance today, what of nationalism itself? Does it have any future? A radical thesis about the prospects of nationalism – and nations – has been advanced by the eminent world historian William McNeill. He argues that civilized societies owed their success to their ability to attract a large supply of varied labour skills. Hence, polyethnicity has been the historical norm, not national unity. The culturally mixed character of premodern empires was reinforced by the periodic incursions of tribesmen envious of their wealth and power, by frequent epidemics which depleted urban populations which in turn had to be replenished from the countryside to meet labour needs, and by long-distance trade organized by often alien merchant communities, with their own scriptural, and hence portable, religions. As a result, civilized societies were cosmopolitan hierarchies of skill, and only outposts of barbarism such as premodern England and Japan could retain their monoethnic character (McNeill 1986: ch. 1).

All this changed after about 1700. The influence of classical humanism and its ideals of political solidarity; the rise of reading publics and vernacular literatures; the rapid growth of indigenous populations in Western Europe, which allowed urban labour needs to be replenished from an ethnically homogenous countryside; and, most important, following the revolution in infantry drill, the emergence of large-scale military participation, which in turn encouraged a new sense of solidarity and fraternity: all these factors came together in the West at the end of the eighteenth century 'to give birth to modern nationalism', with its 'myth of national brotherhood and ethnic unity' (ibid.: 51, 56).

But two world wars have reversed this situation and undone the nationalist ideal. Revulsion against Nazi barbarism, the huge cost and impossibility of waging total war alone, the resulting need to draft thousands of ethnically heterogenous workers and soldiers, the growth of vast transnational enterprises and mass communications, as well as multilateral military blocs, have all undermined the autonomy and power of the national state. The consequence is a return of polyethnic hierarchy, in order once again to meet the urgent need for adequate supplies of skilled labour. In fact, the moment of the barbaric ideal of national unity was not only aberrant in the course of human history, it was ultimately a mirage; the social reality was always one of polyethnic hierarchy, even in the 'nationalist' West.

At first sight, this is a persuasive thesis. Polyethnicity has been, and remains, one of the enduring features of the human condition. But McNeill's thesis is premised on a much greater rupture between *ethnies* and nations, and between ethnicity and nationalism, than historical evidence can support. Leaving aside the presence of several compact *ethnies*, and perhaps nations, in premodern polyethnic ages (and not just on the fringes of 'civilization'), there is no good reason for regarding ethnicity and nationhood as constituting a zero-sum relationship. Though the analytic distinction between them is crucial, in practice, as McNeill admits, ethnicity and nationhood overlap and even sometimes coalesce. As we saw, only the more fanatical organic nationalists desired real cultural homogeneity; most ethnic nationalists were content with a looser unity of culture, will and purpose. Moreover, ethnicity so often forms the cultural basis for the territorial and political claims of nationalism, and most current nationalisms are predicated on the existence of one or more *ethnies*. McNeill fails to see how his ethnic components of postmodern civilization form concentric circles of belonging and loyalty, and that human beings can simultaneously belong, and feel committed, to a series of more inclusive communities, from the family and clan to the *ethnie*, the nation and even, perhaps, to a continental cultural community, with myths of 'brotherhood and unity' operating at each level.

Does this mean, then, that the circle of the nation possesses today no greater importance than those of other cultural communities, that it is just one among our many 'multiple identities' and represents only one choice that individuals may make over their other possible symbolic identifications? And, if so, will the nationalist option wane, as richer and more varied opportunities open up to many more people in a global society and culture? Or is there something much more fundamental and pervasive about the nation, such that the nationalist option will continue to be a recurrent feature of postmodern societies?[9]

The Consumer Society

The idea that postmodern society is also 'post-national', with a concomitant attenuation of national sentiments and a growing disenchantment with nationalist ideologies, is predicated on the thesis of the rise of a cosmopolitan global culture which will increasingly subsume and erode national cultures and identities.

There are two versions of this thesis. The first emphasizes mass consumerism, the material benefits accruing to ever larger numbers of people across the globe, as Western products, technologies and capital seek out fresh consumer markets and gradually raise living standards outside the West. This view draws attention to the mass production of commodities by the huge transnational companies and the growing standardization of consumption patterns wherever living standards permit the purchase of Western goods and services. The flow of commodities and the attractions of consumerism make national boundaries, and national governmental regulations, increasingly powerless and irrelevant. But the key factor in the decline of nationalism is the bypassing of national cultures. The 'cultural imperialism' of mass consumerism dilutes the differences in national cultures, reducing them to packaging and folklore, just as it undermines the capacity to create an autonomous culture and society by creaming off the ablest men and women through emigration and the co-optation of elites into the transnational capitalist economy (see Tomlinson 1991: ch. 3).

There is no doubt that the last fifty years have seen a massive increase in the production and consumption of commodities, and that, as a result, in a variety of fields from architecture and transport to health, education and mass media, cultural similarities outweigh national cultural differences. Mass communications, in particular, have made it possible to reproduce Western stylistic and institutional patterns, along with the wholesale transfer of Western products and activities. At the same time, these reproductions and transfers are organized by national governments and are adapted to the particular assumptions and cultural practices of national communities. Moreover, along with the adoption of Western technologies and communications, including the English language, the elites of many national states, in resisting cultural imperialism, seek to cultivate their own cultural practices, beliefs and styles, and strive for national cultural autonomy while embracing global consumerism. This is most obvious in the spheres of religion, language and literature, and history, but it can also manifest itself in such domains as art and architecture, music (alongside Western popular culture), recreations and family life, as well as in political and legal practices. In these cases, cultural nationalism can coexist with, and feed off, consumer globalism (see Richmond 1984; Schlesinger 1987 and 1991: Part III).

But 'nationalism', as we saw in chapter 2, is more than national sentiment or nationalist ideology. It is also a form of public and politicized culture, based on 'authenticity', as well as a type of political religion seeking to promote the national identity, autonomy and unity of a sacred communion of citizens in their ancestral homeland. In other words, nationalism seeks to create nations in the 'authentic' spirit and image of earlier ethnic and religious communities, but transformed to meet modern geopolitical, economic and cultural conditions. This may involve more or less selection and reinterpretation of earlier myths, symbols, codes, traditions and memories, but always within the parameters and authentic spirit of existing cultures and communities. So, to the degree that they desire to resist imperialist forms of consumerism, the elites of newly created nations can draw on a number of pre-existing cultural resources, which underpin their quest for unity and autonomy. Hence their ability to mobilize their citizens for sacrifice along the road of economic and social development, even while they seek to adopt Western technologies and practices and acquire Western goods and services.

Global Culture?

The second version of the thesis of a 'post-national' order and the withering away of nationalism starts from the notion of a global culture based on electronic mass communications. The information society and mass communications have, it is claimed, created the conditions for a global culture, over a century after Marx and Engels' predictions, one in which a single, cosmopolitan and scientific culture encompasses the globe and delegitimizes all pre-existing ethnic and national cultures. The new digital revolution, and the popularity of computerized information technology, have undermined the attractions of pre-existing cultures and the relevance of non-scientific understandings. Above all, they have made such cultures appear partial, non-rational and 'romantic', and hence, by definition, belonging to another, past epoch of human history, which, with the exception perhaps of its artistic creations, has 'nothing to teach us'. The study of such an epoch, like that of any pre-digital epoch, may have its own attractions, but they are no more relevant to our present cultural concerns than, in Gellner's view, premodern cultures were to a national modernity. On this view, the nation and nationalism belong to a Romantic age, the epoch of modernization, but in an age of mass communications, cosmopolitanism and hybridized culture they no longer concern us.[10]

The age of mass communications is also one of mass migration. McNeill's intermingling of ethnic groups and cultures and Homi Bhabha's hybridization of cultural identities in a post-national epoch chime well with the need to be at home anywhere and everywhere, and therefore to be able to communicate in a medium accessible to all. It is no longer national 'language and culture' in the anonymous, impersonal city that must act as the cement of a modern, industrial society, but information technology and computer literacy, which will overcome all cultural barriers to create the mass communicating, hybridized and postmodern global society. It is these factors, along with the forces of economic interdependence, that led Hobsbawm to decry the current wave of divisive, narrow nationalism which he sees as a temporary and secondary diversion from the true 'movement of history', a reaction of fear in the face of the massive forces of change and of resentment at the ubiquitous presence of the stranger and the drying up of family roots (Hobsbawm 1990: 164, 167–8; cf. A. D. Smith 1998: 123–4, 216–18).

Once again, there is no gainsaying the positive assertions of this thesis. We are undoubtedly experiencing vast changes in the forms, range and intensity of mass communication, though this may be more cumulative than revolutionary. There has also been a massive increase in the rates and range of migration, though again there were proportionate precedents in the last two centuries. But does this amount to the introduction of a new, global type of culture? Or are we dealing simply with a new kind of communication technology and language, a medium without a message?

To say that the creation of 'virtual reality', a world behind the world, as it were, amounts to no more than a technical accomplishment, is certainly to underestimate the intellectual achievement of the revolution in mass communications and its potential. On the other hand, to regard the creation of a new information technology as a different global form of 'culture' is to apply a general word with a definite set of referents to quite different kinds of referent. The term 'culture' refers not just to 'communication' and its technology *tout court*, but to different lifestyles and the expression, through aesthetic styles and media, of human qualities, emotions and modes of activity. In this sense, there were always cultures rather than culture, different historic lifestyles and varied expressions of human qualities, emotions and activities. Such cultures answered to particular collective needs and problems in their specific historical contexts. They administered to the problems of life and death, to grief and injustice, love and loss. They instructed people in the art of coping with life and facing death. They embodied the common sense, the accumulated wisdom and the collective memories of a community across the generations, through specific customs, rituals, morals, manners and artefacts. In this way, they expressed the outlook and emotions of particular collectivities and of their individual members, in contrast to other analogous collectivities.

But in what sense, then, can we speak of a 'global culture'? Certainly, no electronic technology of communications and its virtual creations could answer to the emotional and psychological needs of the 'global citizens' of the future, or instruct them in the art of coping with the joys, burdens, pain and loss that life brings. A global culture of the kind envisaged, at once scientific, affectively neutral and technical, would have to be placeless, timeless and memoryless. An eternal virtual present would remove from view the vistas of past and future, just as the capacity for virtual ubiquity removes all thought of place and location. The coordinates of time and space, so central to nations and nationalism, become meaningless, as compression accelerates to a single point, that of the immediate viewer. The world conjured by technical discourse is here and now, anywhere and everywhere; there is no further need for memory or destiny, ancestry or posterity. Or, for that matter, for direct community; only for the shadowplay of participation at one remove.[11]

But such an austere vision is not what most people have in mind when they speak of a global culture. Marx and Engels, we may recall, looked forward to the fusion of national literatures in a world literature, the coming together of national cultures, not their withering away as irrelevant pre-scientific relics. This means that the skeleton of computerized information technology and the virtual reality it creates must be covered with the flesh and blood of existing cultures; or rather, with selected motifs and elements ('shreds and patches') from those cultures, put together in playful, cynical satire, their original meanings transmuted to fit the ever-elusive present. So, a postmodern and cosmopolitan global culture can only be eclectic, hybrid, fragmentary and presentist, forever being up-dated, forever in search of 'relevance'. Such an esoteric and patchwork culture could only have limited appeal, even when it makes use of popular cultures, and little staying-power and resilience, even though it seeks to avoid pastiche.

Internationalizing Nationalism

The fact that neither a scientific nor an eclectic version of global culture could have much popular resonance and durability suggests that the conditions for a postmodern supersession of nationalism have not yet been realized, and that globalization, far from leading to the supersession of nationalism, may actually reinforce it. This conclusion appears to be supported by three further arguments. The first concerns the consequences for nations and nationalism of the processes of globalization; the second argument returns us to the ethnic basis of nationalism, and its cultural legacy to a postmodern epoch; while the third reinforces ethnic bases by considering the sacred foundations of national identity and their long-term implications.

Let me start with globalization. Anthony Giddens has argued forcefully for the conjunction of a revival of localism alongside, and as a result of, the trend to globalism. The various forces of globalization have the effect of stimulating a new attachment to local areas, issues and problems. This may help to explain the paradox of increasing large-scale supranationalism and fissiparous ethnic nationalism – that is, on the one hand, the emergence of continental associations and communities, and, on the other hand, the proliferation of small-scale ethnic movements of the kind that Hobsbawm decried – alongside other regional and local ecology movements. These are all part of the movement away from class-based politics to the new 'politics of identity', which includes the rise of feminist, regional and green movements. In a postmodern epoch, the result is a layering of politics on three levels: a local ethnic, regional, gender or ecology level; the level of the national state; and, finally, the supranational level of the continental (some would say global) community (Giddens 1991).

There is much to commend in this interpretation. Class-based politics have receded in the West, with the shift away from manufacturing to service-based industries, and there is a whole new roster of political movements to take their place, including a revival of ethnic nationalism. Whether the concept of 'identity politics' is helpful in defining their common features is less certain. For example, gender politics seems quite different from ethnic mobilization, which may cut across gender lines, as the latter may override ethnic divisions. Indeed, the gendering of nations and nationalism, an area of great importance for the study of nationalism, predates globalization and, possibly, even modernity. Moreover, it is not clear that global trends have any necessary connection with the revival (or survival) of local or gender issues; or that ethnic nationalism can be easily fitted into the 'global–local' schema. It seems to me that the ethnic 'revival' and the ethnic level of 'identity politics' require a different kind of explanation; and that the growth of associations at the supranational level, while increasingly a major issue, is nevertheless more of an effect (and perhaps a contributory factor) than a necessary condition of the link between global forces and local ties (see Melucci 1989; Yuval-Davis 1997; Sluga 1998).[12]

It is really at the intermediate level of the national state that the processes of globalization, paradoxically, have their greatest effect. But, once again, the two great forces of globalization, economic interdependence consequent on the operations of the transnational corporations and mass communications resulting from the introduction of information and digital technology, can only accelerate and broaden a preexisting political trend.

We might call this trend the 'internationalization of nationalism'. It takes three forms. In the first place, nationalism and the doctrine of national self-determination have become entrenched as basic principles in the United Nations Charter and in various conventions and treaties, being invoked repeatedly in all kinds of disputes and crises. We might see in this process a trend towards the 'normalization' of nations and nationalism, both as widely diffused and accepted ideologies and as habitual and commensurable collective actors (see Mayall 1990).

Second, nationalist movements have always looked to their predecessors, near or far, for strategy, tactics and inspiration, and often a measure of support. Wave after wave of nationalisms have engulfed successive regions, engendering new claims and making equivalent demands. The 'demonstration effect' of nationalisms has, of course, been greatly assisted by mass communications, political alliances and economic interdependence; but they have only amplified the basic nationalist message.

Finally, insofar as some nationalisms played a crucial causal role in the genesis of the two world wars, and these wars were in turn catalysts for new nationalisms, then it can be said that these earlier nationalisms were instrumental in spreading nationalism-in-general around the globe and making the nation the international norm of political organization. Hence, both directly and indirectly, nationalism has the capacity for replicating itself in every continent and under all kinds of regime.[13]

The effect on the international community has been to expand the already existing framework of 'political pluralism' of sovereign territorial states by adding many new states as a result of the introduction of a second principle of state-formation, namely, that of 'cultural pluralism'. Before, only those states that could claim a large territorial jurisdiction and political sovereignty were admitted to the circle of national states. Now, in addition to territorial jurisdiction and political sovereignty, states must evince a measure of cultural unity and solidarity, and preferably some degree of cultural 'uniqueness' – in terms of language, religion, customs and institutions and cultural history. The processes of globalization, especially mass communications, actually place a much greater premium on international cultural pluralism. They make it much easier for states to inculcate a national culture through the state-run national education system and, likewise, for every member of a community to participate in the resulting political culture – as well as by giving far greater salience and visibility to the differences in national cultures. So, far from diminishing the influence of nationalism or dissolving the fabric of nations, processes of globalization actually disseminate that influence and encourage nations to become more participant and distinctive (A. D. Smith 1995: ch. 6).

Uneven Ethno-histories

But there are deeper reasons, beyond the processes of globalization, which suggest why the conditions for the supersession of nationalism and the dissolution of nations are unlikely
to be met. The first of these reasons stems from the legacy of
premodern ethnicity. This is not simply an argument from
'survivals': that, just as elements of premodern *ethnies* survived into the modern epoch and its nations, so modern
nations and nationalism will persist into a postmodern age.
Rather, it is an argument about the *uneven* distribution of
ethno-history across the globe and its effects on the persistence of nations and nationalism.

   Ethno-history, we may recall, differs from 'history' in that
the latter is concerned with a more or less disinterested and
professional enquiry into the past, whereas the former stands
for the members' own records and memories of a community
and its own rediscovery of an 'authentic' communal past or
pasts. In the latter endeavour, the communal past appears as
a series of original moral lessons and imaginative tableaux,
which vividly illustrate the identity and uniqueness, and the
centrality and essential goodness of the community – whatever the shortcomings of its individual members. Ethno-
history does not address economic and social issues in
themselves, or indeed the development of political institutions. Instead, it focuses on questions of heroism and sacrifice, creativity and renascence, sanctity and worship,
genealogy and tradition, community and leadership. Above
all, it harks back to one or more 'golden age', to which it
seeks, through precept and example, to restore the community in the future. Such golden ages embody the 'essence' of
the community, their 'true' character, but they take many
forms. They may be political and economic, ages of wealth,
power and splendour, such as was witnessed in ancient Egypt
or Inca Peru. They may be religious, times of ascetic faith
and saintliness and wisdom, such as the age of Confucius,
the Upanishads, the Bible and Qur'an. Or they may be
cultural and artistic, when great thinkers, writers and artists
congregated in cities and empires – in ancient Athens and
Alexandria, the medieval Italian city-states or the provinces

of seventeenth-century Netherlands. For later generations of the communities in question, these ages have become canonical; they epitomize all that is great and noble in 'our community', now so sadly missing, but soon to be restored with the nation's rebirth (see A. D. Smith 1997).

But, what if there was no golden age, no heroes and heroines, no great texts or artefacts, by which 'we', the latterday nation, may be guided in the quest for 'our true self'? Are we rendered unworthy of nationhood, and are our aspirations illegitimate? In the nationalist canon, all nations have worthy – and usable – pasts; it is just a matter of finding them. So, it is hardly surprising if in one state after another, one people after another, the same cultural goals and activities are to be found: the formation of historical and literary societies, the quest for material remains and documents, the investigation and cultivation of vernaculars, the recording of the characteristics of native populations, and the rediscovery of ancient folk traditions, customs and rituals. We can find these self-same activities and goals in sub-Saharan Africa and Asia under colonial rule as well as in Europe. The result has been to render the so-called 'unhistorical nations' historical, and restore to them whatever heroes, cultures and even golden ages can be gleaned from extant documents and artefacts. So, the Finns looked back to an age of wisdom and heroism through the rediscovery by Elias Lonnrot of the Karelian ballads which he brought together in the epic *Kalevala*; the Slovaks returned to an early Moravian kingdom under Svatopluk and other kings; the Ukrainians have similarly sought their origins and glorious past in the Cossack traditions and, further back, in Kievan Rus'; while Zimbabweans have found an ancestral age of greatness in the civilization that built the monuments of Great Zimbabwe.[14]

The uneven distribution of recorded authentic ethno-history, with some nations able to boast a 'rich', well-documented, past, while other nations must be content with only a shadowy, submerged past, has spurred continual comparison and emulation. It is not only relative economic deprivation, but also the relative lack of cultural and ethno-symbolic resources that drives nationalisms all over the globe. Nor is this a matter of 'hard data' alone, but of the perception of authenticity on the part of the members of the nation and of outsiders, i.e. of the internal and external recognition of the authentic character of a nation's culture. Given the number of *ethnies* that are potential candidates for nationhood and statehood, and their perceived need to convince themselves and outsiders of their claim, the role of ethno-history and ethnic culture becomes increasingly critical as substantiation and validation of nationhood. Hence, the power of ethno-nationalisms is likely to increase, and their incidence to proliferate.

This conclusion ties in with my earlier contention, reiterated above, that nationalism should be viewed not just as a political ideology, but as a politicized form of culture – one that is public and popular, and 'authentic'. The widespread refashioning of vernacular ethnic cultures into politicized popular, public cultures is one of the central strands of nationalism. Given the number of *ethnies* worldwide, it goes some way to explaining the persistence and proliferation of nationalism at the beginning of the twenty-first century.

Sacred Foundations

But this is only part of the story. It is, even more, in the study of the sacred foundations of nations that we can grasp the continuing hold of national identities and the persistence of nations.

At first glance, such a statement sounds paradoxical. After all, we live in a secular age, at least in the West, one in which material values and preferences have displaced the sense of the sacred and submerged ancient beliefs in transcendental values. The identities that we seek to build are essentially pragmatic; they rest on economic foundations and seek political expression only to encompass and further material interests. Our culture, too, at least at the popular level, is heavily influenced by commercial considerations and lacks any sacred, transcendental dimension, any belief outside the immediate present and its ephemeral expressions. Combined with widespread apathy and cynicism towards political ideals, should we be surprised if the national ideal were to command less loyalty and evoke a greater degree of indifference?

This is not only an issue in the West. There are signs of disaffection with nationalism in other countries outside the West. With the achievement of political independence, there was a waning of nationalist passion, as it became clear that nationalism possessed no formula for rapid economic development, and that it required other ideologies, as well as considerable resources and technologies, to move less developed societies away from their state of economic and cultural dependance.[15]

On the other hand, this realization has not prevented the eruption of nationalist passions based on ethnicity and religion in many postcolonial states, from India and Indonesia to Palestine and Israel, Ethiopia and Angola. Nor has it cooled the nationalist ardour involved in many of the world's major territorial disputes – in Kashmir, Sri Lanka, the Caucasus, the Balkans, the Middle East and the Horn of Africa. In his survey of 'religious nationalisms', Mark Juergensmeyer (1993) drew attention to the failures of secular state nationalisms in the eyes of many, and the attractions of a more radical religiously rooted nationalism bent on societal transformation along the lines of strict interpretations of ancient religious texts and practices. Even if we cannot really speak of a 'new cold war', given the disunity between these various kinds of religious nationalisms, their example certainly presents a serious spiritual and political challenge to frequently ineffective non-Western state nationalisms.

But, even in the West, the sacred bases of the nation have not evaporated. They have certainly been challenged by secular rationalism and have been forced to adapt to social and political changes. But the 'political religion' of secular nationalism continues to draw on older religious motifs for its liturgy, symbolism and myth-making, while presenting itself as the only viable salvation drama in a rationalist age. After all, at the collective level, the exercise of rationalism assumes a measure of cooperation and political solidarity, and this requires a well-defined framework and political arena. For the foreseeable future, the nation – a *community* in possession of its *territory*, and distinguished by its own *history* and *destiny* – undoubtedly provides the most popular and usable framework for political solidarity.

These four basic categories of the nation – community, territory, history and destiny – have in the past and, I would argue, continue in the present to be seen as 'sacred', in the sense of being treated by most members as objects of respect and devotion, and as ends in themselves. This is not to say that aspects of all four have not been called into question. While few have rejected community as such in favour of global cosmopolis, there have been plenty of questions raised about the nature and extent of the homeland, the truth-content and morality of received ethno-history and the alleged virtues and defects of various visions of the community's destiny. Yet, that the world is divided into communities or nations which possess their own territories or homelands, their own histories and their particular destinies – these are beliefs that are rarely questioned by most people. These form what one might term the 'sacred properties' of the nation or, more accurately, the basic properties of the nation conceived as a sacred communion of its members.[16]

These sacred properties, which I outlined in chapter 2, were:

(1) a belief in ethnic election, the idea of the nation as a chosen people, entrusted with a special mission or having an exclusive covenant with the deity;
(2) an attachment to a sacred territory, an ancestral homeland sanctified by saints, heroes and sages, as well as by the tombs and monuments of the ancestors;
(3) shared memories of 'golden ages', as the high points of the nation's ethno-history, ages of material and/or spiritual and artistic splendour;
(4) the cult of the 'glorious dead', and of their heroic self-sacrifice on behalf of the nation and its destiny.

Examples of each of these beliefs, memories and attachments can be found in premodern epochs – in *ethnies*, city-states and empires. Even the cult of the glorious dead has its forerunners in funeral ceremonies and the cult of the ancestors. As George Mosse has demonstrated in the case of Germany, in particular, specifically Christian liturgical and ritual elements were used by the early German nationalists in their demonstrations and celebrations. More generally, the nationalists built upon these traditional religious foundations, selecting and modifying older motifs, symbols and myths for their own political ends. But, at an even more basic level, nationalism as a political religion, as a 'religion of the people', necessarily drew upon these four sacred properties in order to reconstruct and maintain modern national identities (Mosse 1975 and 1994).

I would not wish to claim that all nations were equally suffused by all of these sacred properties. We saw how uneven was the distribution of eventful, well-documented ethno-histories across the globe. This unevenness applies to the other sacred properties as well. In some cases, an attachment to territories held to be sacred became a focal point of the nation's existence, lending it a special character and intensity, as has occurred in cases of protracted territorial disputes. In other cases, shared memories of golden ages came to the fore, acting as summons and guides to collective action. In yet others, the belief in ethnic election, the idea of the community as a chosen people, was paramount, energizing the nation and drawing a sharp line between citizens and outsiders. Perhaps most commonly, the cult of the fallen war heroes and its monuments, together with the ceremonies of commemoration for the 'glorious dead', came to define the nature of the collective bond and the destiny of the citizens.

Now, on the basis of this conception, we may hazard a general hypothesis about the persistence of national identities. Where all four of these sacred properties have been, and still are, widely diffused in an ethno-national population, the resulting national identity has been, and will continue to be, particularly powerful and resilient, creating a sharp boundary between the members and outsiders, and, other things being equal, a reluctance to regard newcomers as full members of the national culture-community. Conversely, where more than one of these sacred properties has become attenuated or is lacking, the power of the national identity was, and is, correspondingly diminished, and its appeal for the population is to that extent undermined vis-à-vis other collective cultural identities. This has tended to encourage a consequent weakening of the sharpness of the social and cultural boundary of the nation, and a greater willingness to accept outsiders, not just as citizens, but as full members of the national community.

Conclusion

At this fundamental level, then, the nation can be regarded as a sacred communion of citizens, and nationalism as a form of 'political religion' with its own scriptures, liturgies, saints and rituals. Yet, there is nothing monolithic or static about either nations or nationalisms. For, just as the traditional religions have periodically undergone processes of change to meet new conditions, so modern national identities are habitually reinterpreted by successive generations; and just as religions contain variant forms, so we find in nationalisms competing myths of national origins and development. Nevertheless, the words with which Durkheim summed up his analysis of religion can also be usefully applied to nations and nationalism:

> Thus there is something eternal in religion which is destined to survive all the particular symbols in which religious thought has successively enveloped itself. There can be no society which does not feel the need of upholding and reaffirming at regular intervals the collective sentiments and collective ideas which make up its unity and its personality. (Durkheim 1915: 427)

So long, therefore, as the sacred foundations of the nation persist, and secular materialism and individualism have not undermined the central beliefs in a community of history and destiny, so long is nationalism – as political ideology, as public culture and as political religion – destined to flourish, and so long will national identity continue to provide one of the basic building-blocks of the contemporary world order.

Notes

Chapter 1   Concepts

1   For fuller discussions of these key terms, see Zernatto (1944), Snyder (1954) and Kemilainen (1964).

2   Definitions of nationalism that equate it with national sentiment can be found in Michelat and Thomas (1966), Kohn (1967a: ch. 1) and Seton-Watson (1977: ch. 1).

3   For the strategies and tactics of nationalist movements, see Breuilly (1993) and Esman (1994). The nationalist goals and tactics of stateless nations in the West are analysed by Guibernau (1999).

4   For an analysis of nationalism as mainly a discursive formation, see Calhoun (1997); see also Brubaker (1996).

5   While there is no general study of national symbolism, the essays in Hobsbawm and Ranger (1983) and the work of Mosse (1975 and 1990), are of great value. See also Hedetoft (1995: Part I, ch. 4), and the essays in the great opus on French 'sites of memory', edited by Nora (1997–8, esp. Vol. III).

6   Most 'anti-colonial' nationalisms were ideological movements of minorities among ethnically heterogeneous populations thrown together by colonial administrations, as in Nigeria or India. Yet, though they possessed no national basis, on the European model, these elites aimed to create one. Theirs were 'nations of intent' (Rotberg 1967). See also Chatterjee (1986).

7   Here, the distinction made by Walker Connor (1994: 202) between historical and *felt* reality, is useful; what counts is not what is, but what is felt to be, the case.

8   For the idea of the nation and national character predating the ideology of nationalism by at least a century, see the richly detailed studies of Kemilainen (1964) and Greenfeld (1992: chs 1–2).

9   For valuable discussions of the problems of defining the concept of the nation, see Deutsch (1966: ch. 1), Rustow (1967) and Connor (1994: ch. 4).

10 On diasporas, see Cohen (1997). In fact, most *ethnies* reside in their own territories, but in the premodern past these were often not bordered. Other *ethnies* were both resident in an ancestral homeland and scattered, as was the case with some of the Ottoman *millets*; see Armstrong (1982: ch. 7).

11 For these definitions, see A. D. Smith (1986: ch. 2; 1991: ch. 1). See also Motyl (1999: chs 4–5)

12 It is not simply that nations are a delocalized and politicized form of *ethnie*, as Akzin (1964) had claimed; *ethnies* may, after all, be quite extensive and populous, and may be organized in political form, as ethnic states. Rather, what differentiates the nation from the *ethnie* is the *type* of (public) culture, (single, territorial) economy and legal order (common rights and duties for members). For an elaboration of these points, see A. D. Smith (2000a: ch. 3), and ch. 5 below.

13 For the role of modern diaspora communities in international politics, see Sheffer (1986); and on the modern, multilocal Armenian diaspora, see Panossian (2000).

14 Here, we may distinguish two kinds of 'failed' nationalism: a failure of an ethnic category or *ethnie* to develop a strong nationalist movement; and a failure of that nationalism to achieve its political goals. Occitanians or Copts might be given as examples of the former failure, while Kurds and Tamils would (to date) exemplify the latter kind of 'failure'. See A. D. Smith (1983: ch. 9).

15 For the term 'state-nation', see Zartmann (1964). Horowitz (1985: ch. 2) describes the effects for ethnic groups of the new territorial boundaries created by colonial powers.

16 This is the approach taken by Fishman (1980) in his original analysis of the profound bonds of ethnicity and language in Eastern Europe, which in his view modernist approaches tend to obscure. For a critique, see A. D. Smith (1998: 159–61).

17 The need for this kind of intergenerational analysis is the central point made by John Armstrong (1982: ch. 1) and by historical ethno-symbolists in general.

Chapter 2 Ideologies

1 For intellectual and moral critiques of nationalist ideology, see Minogue (1967), Dunn (1978: ch. 3) and Parekh (1995).

2 For some, albeit incomplete, surveys of early nationalist thinkers, see Baron (1960), Kohn (1965, 1967a and 1967b) and Viroli (1995); cf. also Sluga (1998).

3 This follows, of course, from the finite nature of nations; as Anderson (1991) reminds us, there must always be some people who stand outside the nation.

4 We may ask: were 'national communisms' communisms with a national direction or nationalisms with a communist direction? On which, see Kautsky (1962: Introduction and essay by Lowenthal).

5 For an argument which highlights the growing importance of stateless nations as political actors, see Guibernau (1999).

6 On irredentism in European history, see Seton-Watson (1977: ch. 3) and Alter (1989). On irredentism and borders in Africa, see Asiwaju (1985); and for Caucasian irredentisms and separatisms, see Wright, Goldenberg and Schofield (1996). For the differences between irredentism and separatism, see Horowitz (1992).

7 On the ideas of Fichte, Jahn and Muller, see Kedourie (1960) and Kohn (1965). Of course, the ideas of fraternal love and unity were paramount concerns of the *patriots* in the French Revolution; see Schama (1989: ch. 12).

8 On Herder, see the excellent studies of Barnard (1965) and Berlin (1976). On the metaphors of 'national awakening', see Pearson (1993); the uses of scholarly disciplines by nationalisms are explored in A. D. Smith (1986: ch. 7).

9 Nationalist myths of origins and descent are analysed in the essays in Hosking and Schöpflin (1997) and by A. D. Smith (1999a: ch. 2). See also the fascinating account of the Hungarian model of 'authentic' peasant culture by Tamas Hofer: 'The ethnic model of peasant cultures', in Sugar (1980).

10 For the influence of nationalism on archaeology, see Diaz-Andreu and Champion (1996) and Jones (1997). A penetrating account of the uses of history and archaeology to create an Israeli national tradition is given by Zerubavel (1995).

11 The concept of group worth is explored by Horowitz (1985: chs 4–5). For some Asian examples, see the essays in Tønnesson and Antlov (1996) and in Leifer (2000).

12 This raises the interesting question of whether city-states like Athens, Sparta, Florence and Venice might be regarded as

small-scale nations, their 'patriotism' really a civic type of nationalism, indeed its prototype (see Cohen 2000). For an attempt to describe the differences between republican patriotism and (German ethno-cultural) nationalism, which is not altogether successful, see Viroli (1995); cf. Fondation Hardt (1962) and Finley (1986: ch. 7) on some contextual differences in the case of the ancient Greek *polis*.

13   See the classic analysis in Matossian (1962). For the Danish case, see Ulfe Ostergard: 'Peasants and Danes: The Danish national identity and political culture', in Eley and Suny (1996).

14   This has been a relatively neglected field until the 1990s. But, see the useful collections by Hooson (1994) and Herb and Kaplan (1999); and the striking analysis of Canadian and Swiss ethnoscapes in Kaufman and Zimmer (1998).

15   Such romantic, populist elements can be found even in civic and territorial nationalisms – for example, in the United States and Mexico; see Tuveson (1968) and Ades (1989), and the fascinating account of Mexican ethnic cultures in Gutierrez (1999).

16   For Durkheim and nationalism, see Mitchell (1931). On the role of commemorative ceremonies for the fallen, especially in Germany, see Mosse (1975, 1990 and 1994).

17   For an analysis of typologies of nationalism, see A. D. Smith (1983: chs 8–9); cf. also Plamenatz (1976).

18   On the ideal of Germania, see Llobera (1994: Part I); and on Weber's nationalism, see Beetham (1974). The transition from a linguistic to a more racial German nationalism is analysed in Kohn (1965) and Bracher (1973).

19   For a critique of Kohn's dichotomy, see Hutchinson (1987: ch. 1); see also A. D. Smith (1983: ch. 8).

20   See Hayes (1931) and Snyder (1976); cf. Tilly (1975: Introduction and Conclusion) and Seton-Watson (1977: ch. 1).

Chapter 3   Paradigms

1   On these Revolutionary fêtes, see Herbert (1972); see also Crow (1985: ch. 7) for the art of David and others before and during the Revolution, and its links with politics.

2   The Enlightenment background and influence on the Revolution is explored in Baker (1988). On the French Revolution and nationalism, see Cobban (1963), Kohn (1967b) and O'Brien (1988b).

3   On citizenship in France from the Revolution, see Brubaker (1992). The gendering of nations and nationalism from the Revolution and Romanticism is well documented and analysed by Sluga (1998).

4   On Rousseau and nationalism, see Cobban (1964) and Cohler (1970). For the return to classical models in France, see Cobban (1963: 162–9) and Kennedy (1989: ch. 4).

5   Actually, sociological modernism holds that (a) nationalism is both recent and novel, (b) nations and national states are also recent and novel and (c) all these national phenomena are products of modernity and/or modernization. For a much fuller discussion, see A. D. Smith (1998: Part I).

6   The recent work of Nairn (1997) accords more weight to social psychology and cultural anthropology, notably to the cultural and social power of nationality. Hechter (1992 and 2000), meanwhile, has shifted to a more political, rational choice model of nationalism.

7   Other scholars who stress the power and role of nationalist ideology include Kapferer (1988), O'Brien (1988a), Juergensmeyer (1993) and Van der Veer (1994).

8   Expressions of the recent burgeoning of interest in the connections between nationalism and archaeology, and the political context of archaeology, include Kohl and Fawcett (1995), Diaz-Andreu and Champion (1996), and Diaz-Andreu and A. D. Smith (2001).

9   Though analytically separable, there is, in practice, no hard-and-fast line between continuous and recurrent perennialism. In the work of certain scholars, such as John Armstrong (1982), we can find both types: tracing the origins of particular nations like the Persians or Armenians, combined with an investigation of recurrent nationhood and nations in the medieval Middle East and Europe; on the one hand, the slow emergence of modern national identities from medieval roots and, on the other hand, the constant formation and re-formation of ethnic and national identities over *la longue durée*.

10 For a critique of nationalist naturalism and essentialism, see Penrose (1995); cf. also Brubaker (1996: ch. l) and, in the context of a constructionist and feminist critique of nationalism, Yuval-Davis (1997).

11 For an introduction to primordialism, see Stack (1986: Introduction). The idea of territory as a life-enhancing power is proposed by Grosby (1995); cf. the critique of primordialism by Eller and Coughlan (1993), the reply by Grosby (1994) and the discussion in A. D. Smith (1998: ch. 7).

12   There is a vast literature on ethnicity in the United States, and on instrumentalism. See especially, Herberg (1960); Glazer and Moynihan (1963: Introduction); Bell (1975); Gans (1979); Okamura (1981); and Scott (1990).

13   This is the particular concern of John Armstrong's (1982) path-breaking study of ethnic identity in premodern Islamic and Christian civilizations.

14   For a classic early analysis of this 'onion' character of ethnicity and nationhood, through a detailed study of colonial Nigeria, see Coleman (1958, esp. Appendix).

15   Nevertheless, the subjective elements should not be over-stressed. *Ethnies* are treated by ethno-symbolists as sociocultural formations which require sociological explanations; they constitute felt and acted realities, not primarily discursive formations. For nationalism as a form of behaviour, see Beissinger (1998).

Chapter 4   Theories

1   Recently, Michael Hechter (2000) has advanced a theory of nationalism in terms of the effects of the transition from indirect to direct rule, marrying a rational choice to a political structure approach within the overall modernist paradigm. Other recent approaches are considered in chapter 6, below. All of them operate within a modernist paradigm, which they seek, in various ways, to surpass.

2   For Kedourie, both Kant's and Herder's doctrines were products of an Enlightenment quest for certainty and perfection. But, in fact, Herder's ideas on cultural diversity and authenticity, along with Rousseau's naturalism, represented a critique of Enlightenment rationalism and universalism; see Barnard (1969) and Berlin (1999: ch. 3).

3   For fuller critiques, see Hutchinson (1987: ch. 1) and A. D. Smith (1998: ch. 2). A recent incisive assessment of Gellner's theory, taking his later writings into account, is O'Leary (1998). See also the other evaluations of Gellner's theory, from a modernist standpoint, in Hall (1998).

4   But, see Nairn's later, more social psychological and anthropological analysis in Nairn (1997, esp. Introduction and ch. 5).

5   For an account of recent nationalisms in Europe since 1989 which is much indebted to Gellner's theory, see Dieckhoff (2000).

6   Kedourie's attempt to derive modern nationalism from antinomian medieval Christian millennialism seems to me mis-

taken; see A. D. Smith (1979: ch. 2). But, by linking national-ism to religion, Kedourie opened the way to a more satisfac-tory account of the varieties of nationalisms and the passions they evoke.

7   Hechter gives as examples the interesting cases of the Amish and the Gypsies, both of them relatively closed communities, whether by choice or necessity (Hechter 1988: 275–6). For the Gypsies, see Kenrick and Puxon (1972).

8   But one can think of counter-cases, for example, the Palestin-ian *intifada* against a strong Israeli state, or the Irish national-ist reaction to strong British repression after the 1916 Easter Rising. Moreover, it was the transition to a weaker, less cen-tralized and collegial system of rule in Yugoslavia after Tito's death in 1980 that paved the way for ethno-nationalist vio-lence; see Ramet (1996, esp. Parts I and IV).

9   Here, again, the Yugoslav case comes to mind: could one explain the intensity of nationalisms and their violence without taking mutual memories of the Second World War into ac-count, including Serb memories of Ustasha massacres? For the role of memory in Ireland, see Lyons (1979) and Hutchinson (1987: chs 2–4).

10   This is a point also made forcefully by Joshua Fishman (1980). Fishman stresses the ubiquitous and durable character of 'unmobilized ethnicity' – against modernist misunderstandings of nationalism. See also Nash (1989).

11   Here, Connor's argument owed a good deal to Eugene Weber's (1979) thesis that it was only at the end of the nineteenth century, as a result of the modernization policies of the Third Republic, that the great mass of people in France – the peas-ants – became truly French in culture and outlook. But, even granting this, it does not follow that we cannot speak of a French nation before the late nineteenth century. Institution-ally, culturally and politically, a French 'nation' had come into being well before that date, and was alive and active in the consciousness and behaviour of the educated classes at least since the sixteenth century. See, for example, Hastings (1997: ch. 4); and for a still earlier period, Beaune (1985).

12   In their different ways, Bell (1975) and Brass (1991) do attempt to incorporate emotion and symbolism into a broadly instru-mentalist framework, balancing 'interest' and 'affect'.

13   For another state-centred modernist approach, see Tilly (1975: Introduction and Conclusion). For more geopolitical ap-proaches, see Orridge (1982) and Mayall (1990). McCrone (1998: ch. 5) gives a balanced account of the 'state and nation' debates.

14   There are also the early cases of Irish and Welsh 'nations', which, though never really united in a single state, possessed distinct linguistic cultures, territories and some common legal rights for many members, as well as a clear sense of the outsider; see Hastings (1997: ch. 3). There is also the interesting case of Switzerland, which, since at least the fifteenth century, was loosely united in the Old Confederation (*Eidgenossenschaft*), founded in the 1291 Oath of the Rütli as an instrument of resistance to the encroachments of the Habsburg rulers on their former liberties; on which, see Steinberg (1976) and Im Hof (1991). See also the thought-provoking analysis of 'ethnic' and 'civic' components of Swiss national identity, in Zimmer (1999).

15   See Kohn (1967a: ch. 4) for a description of incipient German national sentiment among the Renaissance humanists, and Llobera (1994: Part I) for an analysis of the medieval formation of a domain of 'Germania'.

16   For very different accounts of German and Afrikaner nationalisms and their myths, see Kohn (1965) and Cauthen (1997 and 2000). For the United States and its myth of a providential mission ('manifest destiny'), see Tuveson (1968), O'Brien (1988a) and Greenfeld (1992: ch. 5).

17   But equally, for Hutchinson (1987: ch. 1), cultural and political nationalisms must not be conflated; that is a key element in his critique of Kedourie.

18   For a more extended argument on the respective weight of states and *ethnies*, see A. D. Smith (1998: chs 4, 8).

19   Unlike Hobsbawm, Anderson thinks that nations and nationalism are not destined to pass away in a postmodern epoch. But such an assertion is not easily derived from the modernist elements of his theory. It is necessary to appeal to the other elements or 'fatalities' in his approach – fear of oblivion and global linguistic Babel – to make sense of this prediction. See Anderson (1999).

20   Anderson's emphasis on the cognitive aspects of nationalism has encouraged others to see in nationalism primarily a 'discursive formation' leading to particular political practices and categorizations; see especially Brubaker (1996) and Calhoun (1997). For a more historical and structural use of Anderson, see Kitromilides (1989).

21   Hobsbawm's account has proved highly influential; see for example Ram's (1995) account of Israeli nationalism, and Kreis's (1991) account of late nineteenth-century Swiss nationalism. For further analysis, see chapter 5, below.

22 For elements of Greek continuity, at least from the Byzantine epoch, see Campbell and Sherrard (1968: ch. 1) and Armstrong (1982: 174–81). See also Roudometov (1998).

23 For analyses of 'golden age' myths, see Hosking and Schöpflin (1997). Fuller statements of my own ethno-symbolic approach can be found in A. D. Smith (1999a: Introduction; 2000a: ch. 3).

24 Of course, there are problems with the concept of ethnicity, and its often elusive quality has led some, particularly among anthropologists, to avoid it altogether, and others to regard it as of little explanatory value for nations and nationalism; see, for example, Poole (1999: 34–43). Such avoidance or relegation may have something to do with the pernicious political uses to which ethnic sentiments have been put as much as with serious intellectual doubts, but, given participant action and passion, this seems to be both unrealistic and a counsel of despair. While ethnicity on its own cannot provide an 'explanation' of the origins and appeal of nations and nationalism, myths of common origin and ethnic attachments must figure prominently in an historical approach to nations and nationalism. For a lucid discussion of different anthropological approaches to ethnicity, see Eriksen (1993).

Chapter 5   Histories

1 For the second wave of European nationalisms, see Trevor-Roper (1961). The ideological varieties of nationalism are discussed by Hayes (1931) and Kohn (1967a).

2 For the earlier version, see Snyder (1954) and Kohn (1955); and for the later, see Snyder (1976), Alter (1989) and Schulze (1996).

3 Gellner (1973) offers an original sociological explanation for the size and scale of nations; see also the revealing examples in the Habsburg empire given by Argyle (1976).

4 For this general social evolutionary trend, see Parsons (1966). The model of 'nation-building' and citizenship is described in Deutsch and Foltz (1963) and Bendix (1996).

5 Hobsbawm's approach has influenced a number of scholars (see above, chapter 4, note 21). To the aforementioned examples, we may add Kitromilides (1998) on the relatively recent identification of Greece with Byzantium by Greek historians, and Zerubavel's (1995) analysis of the uses to which Israelis have put the Bar-Kochba revolt and the Masada myth.

6   On these varieties of nationalisms, see Kohn (1967a), Snyder (1976) and Gilbert (1998).

7   There is an implicit criticism here of Greenfeld's limited medieval usage (see Greenfeld 1992: Introduction). More important were the 'national' divisions at Church Councils, which reflected wider medieval usage.

8   This is the main argument put forward by Breuilly (1993) in favour of modernism; and it is one stressed by Bendix (1996) and implicitly by Connor (1994: ch. 9).

9   The teleological element in Seton-Watson's approach has been criticized by Susan Reynolds (1984: ch. 8). Medieval communities, in her eyes, should not be retrospectively classified as embryonic nations, with their boundaries and sentiments as the first stages of a predetermined development towards modern nations, but as communities of custom, law, descent and government, or *regna*, with their popular sentiments, therefore, being termed 'regnal'. Nevertheless, there remains a clear parallel between these early medieval communities and kingdoms, on the one hand, and modern nations and national sentiments, on the other; and we are left wondering about their possible relationships. See the comment by Llobera (1994: 86): 'Modern nationalisms are re-creations of medieval realities; in fact, they can only be successful if they are rooted in the medieval past, even if the links with it may often be tortuous and twisted.'

10   See Hastings (1997: 9): 'Understanding nations and nationalism will only be advanced when any inseparable bonding of them to the modernisation of society is abandoned.'

11   For interesting studies of other cases of medieval 'nations', see Knoll (1993) on fifteenth-century Polish national consciousness, Im Hof (1991) on the role of earlier founding myths recorded in the chronicles of the fifteenth- and sixteenth-century Swiss Confederation, and Webster (1997) on the growth of Scottish national sentiment after the Wars of Independence. See also the stimulating analysis by Ichijo (1998) of contemporary Scots' uses of premodern Scottish identity.

12   Other studies stress this formative period of English nationalism; see Kohn (1940) and Corrigan and Sayer (1985). For a more cautious view that stresses the complexity of relationships between politics, religion and ethnicity in the British Isles during this period, see Kidd (1999). For the subsequent growth of a *British* nationalism, see Colley (1992).

13   Hastings argues, like Gellner, that Islam is inhospitable to nationalism, because its concept of the all-embracing *umma* transcends the nation, and its insistence on the sacred status of

Qur'anic Arabic rules out any sanctification of vernacular languages. Against this, we may note the way in which the Catholic Church and Christendom transcended and impeded the rise of nations, and how Vulgate Latin occupied a similar place to Arabic before the Reformation. Nor did the primacy of the Arabs prevent a renaissance of Persian ethnicity and language from the eleventh century, or the retention of Turkish and other ethnicities within Islam. Besides, the ulema supported rival Islamic dynastic states which often fed and were reinforced by pre-existing ethnic sentiments. See Armstrong (1982: ch. 3) and Frye (1975).

14 On Hastings' criteria, we might also include the Maronites, Copts and Samaritans in the canon of 'nations' in late antiquity; on which, see Atiyah (1968), Purvis (1968) and A. D. Smith (1986: ch. 5).

15 For a different view of Buddhism as a political religion, see Sarkisyanz (1964) and D. E. Smith (1974); and on medieval Sri Lankan ethnicity and religion and its links with modern nationalism, see Roberts (1993) and Subaratnam (1997).

16 On the problematic nature of 'ethnicity', see chapter 4, note 24 above. For other critiques, see the essays in Wilmsen and McAllister (1996) and Calhoun (1997).

17 For accounts of the formation of Wales and Ireland, see Williams (1985) and de Paor (1986).

18 It would be more accurate to say that, in these cases, state and nation developed *pari passu*, mutually reinforcing each other. For the mental 'roadblocks' of modernism and ethnocentrism, see Fishman (1980).

19 Gellner, too, was prepared to concede the early emergence of nationalist sentiment in England (Gellner 1983: 91–2, footnote); cf. also his view (in Gellner 1997: 51) that in a large area of Western Europe the union of culture and polity was established long before the logic of modern (industrial) society required it. This suggests that the reason is not some peculiarity of England or the British Isles, but the geopolitical and cultural mapping of Western Europe; on which, see Orridge (1982).

20 On the Jewish diaspora and its Ashkenazic and Sephardic divisions, see Seltzer (1980), Elazar (1986), Kedourie (1992) and Goldberg (1996).

21 On the close historic links between territory and nationalism, see the essays in Hooson (1994) and Herb and Kaplan (1999). Schama (1995, esp. chs 1–4) offers a suggestive account of memory and landscape. For a broad-ranging study of Russia,

see Bassin (1991); and, for sacred territories, see A. D. Smith (1999b).
22 A view also found, at least for the ancient Jews, in Brandon (1967) and Stern (1972). For a more general recurrent perennialism, see Armstrong (1982).
23 See the fuller discussion in A. D. Smith (2000a: ch. 2).
24 For more on these peoples in the ancient world, see Wiseman (1973) and A. D. Smith (1986: chs 2–5). On ancient and medieval Iran, see Frye (1966 and 1975); and for the rediscovery and revival of Pharaonic Egypt, see Gershoni and Jankowski (1987). On diasporas generally, see Armstrong (1976) and Cohen (1997).
25 For these public rituals and laws in ancient Babylonia and Israel, see Frankfort (1948) and Zeitlin (1984).

Chapter 6   Prospects

1 For 'nation-building', see Deutsch (1966). The uses of national self-determination in decolonization are discussed by Mayall (1990, esp. ch. 4).
2 There is a large literature on the so-called 'ethnic revival' in Europe in the 1960s and 1970s; see, inter alia, Esman (1977), Stone (1979), A. D. Smith (1981a) and Guibernau (1996).
3 On the role of nationalism and ethnicity in the successor states of the Soviet Union, see Bremmer and Taras (1993) and Suny (1993). On Eastern Europe, see Glenny (1990) and on the Balkans, see Ramet (1996). For a recent original theoretical analysis of the role of ethnicity and the state in contemporary European, especially Central and Eastern European, nationalisms, see Schöpflin (2000).
4 For fuller discussions, see Giddens (1985) and A. D. Smith (1995: ch. 4).
5 See the argument in Soysal (1994) that, though immigrants are accorded more or less the same human rights and benefits as citizens in European states as a result of a host of international agreements, these rights and benefits are organized by, and according to the practices of, each national state. See also Preece (1998) for the effects on ethnic minorities in Europe.
6 For fuller discussions of European cultural 'identity' and political unification, see A. D. Smith (1992), Schlesinger (1992) and Pieterse (1995), and the critique by Delanty (1995).
7 See also Bhabha (1994). For the idea of new, more optional and symbolic ethnicities in a multicultural society, see Hall (1992). See also the symposium on David Miller's work, edited

by O'Leary (1996). For a strong liberal rejoinder to multiculturalist arguments, see Barry (1999).

8 For concepts of 'France' during the Dreyfus Affair, see Kedward (1965), and, more generally on French nationalisms, Kohn (1967b), Eugene Weber (1991) and Gildea (1994).

9 On symbolic ethnicity, see Gans (1979). For the idea of multiple, situational identities, see Coleman (1958: Appendix), Okamura (1981) and Balibar and Wallerstein (1991).

10 On the technological revolutions of postmodernity, see Harvey (1989); see also Giddens (1991).

11 These paragraphs are based on A. D. Smith (1995: ch. 1) and the essays in Featherstone (1990).

12 There is a large and growing literature on gender and nationalism; see especially Yuval-Davis and Anthias (1989) and the special issue edited by Kandiyoti (2000).

13 On war and nationalism, see Marwick (1974) and A. D. Smith (1981b); for war sacrifices and commemoration, see Mosse (1990), Gillis (1994) and Winter (1995, esp. ch. 4). On the new wars fought by particularistic groups for specific ends, see Kaldor (1999, esp. ch. 4).

14 On the uses of the *Kalevala* by the Finns, see Branch (1985: Introduction); for the Slovak revival, see Brock (1976); for the history of Kievan Rus' and the recovery of the Cossack inheritance, see Subtelny (1994: chs 1–2, 13); and for the politics of Great Zimbabwe, see Chamberlin (1979: 27–35).

15 A good example of such disaffection, especially among some intellectuals, is provided by the rise of the new post-Zionist mood in Israel, on which see Ram (1998), though it is doubtful whether it is widely shared by the population at large. A similar divide between elites and the majority can be discerned in attitudes to 'Europe', on which see Delanty (1995).

16 This thesis is more fully discussed in A. D. Smith (2000b). For religion and nationalism, see Armstrong (1997).

References

Ades, Dawn (ed.) (1989): *Art in Latin America: The Modern Era, 1820–1980*. London: South Bank Centre, Hayward Gallery.

Akzin, Benjamin (1964): *State and Nation*. London: Hutchinson.

Alter, Peter (1989): *Nationalism*. London: Edward Arnold.

Anderson, Benedict (1991): *Imagined Communities: Reflections on the Origins and Spread of Nationalism*, 2nd edn. London: Verso.

Anderson, Benedict (1999): 'The goodness of nations', in Peter Van der Veer and Hartmut Lehmann (eds), *Nation and Religion: Perspectives on Europe and Asia*. Princeton: Princeton University Press.

Argyle, W. J. (1969): 'European nationalism and African tribalism', in P. H. Gulliver (ed.), *Tradition and Transition in East Africa*. London: Pall Mall Press.

Argyle, W. J. (1976): 'Size and scale in the development of nationalist movements', in Anthony D. Smith (ed.), *Nationalist Movements*. London: Macmillan, and New York: St Martin's Press.

Armstrong, John (1976): 'Mobilized and proletarian diasporas'. *American Political Science Review* 70: 393–408.

Armstrong, John (1982): *Nations before Nationalism*. Chapel Hill: University of North Carolina Press.

Armstrong, John (1995): 'Towards a theory of nationalism: consensus and dissensus', in Sukumar Periwal (ed.), *Notions of Nationalism*. Budapest: Central European University Press.

Armstrong, John (1997): 'Religious nationalism and collective violence'. *Nations and Nationalism* 3, 4: 597–606.

Asiwaju, A. I. (ed.) (1985): *Partitioned Africans: Ethnic Relations across Africa's International Boundaries, 1884–1984.* London: C. Hurst and Company.

Atiyah, A. S. (1968): *A History of Eastern Christianity.* London: Methuen.

Baker, Keith Michael (1988): *Inventing the French Revolution.* Cambridge: Cambridge University Press.

Balibar, Etienne and Wallerstein, Immanuel (1991): *Race, Nation, Class.* London: Verso.

Barnard, F. M. (ed.) (1965): *Herder's Social and Political Thought: From Enlightenment to Nationalism.* Oxford: Clarendon Press.

Barnard, F. M. (1969): 'Culture and political development: Herder's suggestive insights'. *American Political Science Review* 62: 379–97.

Baron, Salo (1960): *Modern Nationalism and Religion.* New York: Meridian Books.

Barry, Brian (1999): 'The limits of cultural politics', in Desmond Clarke and Charles Jones (eds), *The Rights of Nations: Nations and Nationalism in a Changing World.* Cork: Cork University Press.

Barth, Fredrik (ed.) (1969): *Ethnic Groups and Boundaries.* Boston: Little, Brown and Co.

Bassin, Mark (1991): 'Russia between Europe and Asia: the ideological construction of geographical space'. *Slavic Review* 50, 1: 1–17.

Baynes, N. H. and Moss, H. St. L. B. (eds) (1969): *Byzantium: An Introduction to East Roman Civilization.* Oxford, London and New York: Oxford University Press.

Beaune, Colette (1985): *Naissance de la Nation France.* Paris: Editions Gallimard.

Beetham, David (1974): *Max Weber and the Theory of Modern Politics.* London: Allen and Unwin.

Beissinger, Mark (1998): 'Nationalisms that bark and nationalisms that bite: Ernest Gellner and the substantiation of nations', in John Hall (ed.), *The State of the Nation: Ernest Gellner and the Theory of Nationalism.* Cambridge: Cambridge University Press.

Bell, Daniel (1975): 'Ethnicity and Social Change', in Nathan Glazer and Daniel P. Moynihan (eds), *Ethnicity: Theory and Experience.* Cambridge, MA: Harvard University Press.

Bendix, Reinhard (1996) [1964]: *Nation-building and Citizenship*, enlarged edn. New Brunswick, NJ: Transaction Publishers.

Berlin, Isaiah (1976): *Vico and Herder.* London: Hogarth Press.

Berlin, Isaiah (1999): *The Roots of Nationalism* (ed. Henry Hardy). London: Chatto and Windus.

Bhabha, Homi (ed.) (1990): *Nation and Narration*. London and New York: Routledge.

Bhabha, Homi (1994): 'Anxious nations, nervous states', in Jean Copjec (ed.), *Supposing the Subject*. London: Verso.

Billig, Michael (1995): *Banal Nationalism*. London: Sage.

Binder, Leonard (1964): *The Ideological Revolution in the Middle East*. New York: John Wiley.

Blyden, Edward (1893): 'Study and Race'. *Sierra Leone Times*, 3 June 1893.

Bracher, Karl (1973): *The German Dictatorship: The Origins, Structure and Effects of National Socialism*. Harmondsworth: Penguin.

Branch, Michael (ed.) (1985): *Kalevala, The Land of Heroes*, trans. W. F. Kirby. London: The Athlone Press, and New Hampshire: Dover Books.

Brandon, S. G. F. (1967): *Jesus and the Zealots*. Manchester: Manchester University Press.

Brass, Paul (1979): 'Elite groups, symbol manipulation and ethnic identity among the Muslims of North India', in David Taylor and Malcolm Yapp (eds), *Political Identity in South Asia*. London and Dublin: Curzon Press.

Brass, Paul (1991): *Ethnicity and Nationalism*. London: Sage.

Bremmer, Ian and Taras, Ray (eds) (1993): *Nations and Politics in the Soviet Successor States*. Cambridge: Cambridge University Press.

Breuilly, John (1993): *Nationalism and the State*, 2nd edn. Manchester: Manchester University Press.

Breuilly, John (1996a): *The Formation of the First German Nation-State, 1800–71*. Basingstoke: Macmillan.

Breuilly, John (1996b): 'Approaches to nationalism', in Gopal Balakrishnan (ed.), *Mapping the Nation*. London and New York: Verso.

Brock, Peter (1976): *The Slovak National Awakening*. Toronto: University of Toronto Press.

Brown, David (1994): *The State and Ethnic Politics in Southeast Asia*. London and New York: Routledge.

Brubaker, Rogers (1992): *Citizenship and Nationhood in France and Germany*. Cambridge, MA: Harvard University Press.

Brubaker, Rogers (1996): *Nationalism Reframed: Nationhood and the National Question in the New Europe*. Cambridge: Cambridge University Press.

Calhoun, Craig (1997): *Nationalism*. Buckingham: Open University Press.

Campbell, John and Sherrard, Philip (1968): *Modern Greece*. London: Ernest Benn.

Carr, Edward (1945): *Nationalism and After*. London: Macmillan.

Cauthen, Bruce (1997): 'The myth of divine election and Afrikaner ethnogenesis', in Geoffrey Hosking and George Schöpflin (eds), *Myths and Nationhood*. London: Macmillan.

Cauthen, Bruce (2000): 'Confederate and Afrikaner Nationalism: Myth, Identity and Gender in Comparative Perspective', unpublished Ph.D. thesis. University of London.

Chamberlin, E. R. (1979): *Preserving the Past*. London: J. M. Dent and Sons.

Chatterjee, Partha (1986): *Nationalist Thought and the Colonial World*. London: Zed Books.

Chatterjee, Partha (1993): *The Nation and Its Fragments*. Cambridge: Cambridge University Press.

Cobban, Alfred (1963): *A History of Modern France, 1715–99*, vol. I, 3rd edn. Harmondsworth: Penguin.

Cobban, Alfred (1964): *Rousseau and the Modern State*, 2nd edn. London: Allen and Unwin.

Cohen, Edward (2000): *The Athenian Nation*. Princeton: Princeton University Press.

Cohen, Robin (1997): *Global Diasporas, An Introduction*. London: UCL Press.

Cohler, Anne (1970): *Rousseau and Nationalism*. New York: Basic Books.

Coleman, James (1958): *Nigeria, Background to Nationalism*. Berkeley and Los Angeles: University of California Press.

Colley, Linda (1992): *Britons, Forging the Nation, 1707–1837*. New Haven, CT: Yale University Press.

Connor, Walker (1972): 'Nation-building or nation-destroying?'. *World Politics* XXIV, 3: 319–55.

Connor, Walker (1994): *Ethno-Nationalism: The Quest for Understanding*. Princeton: Princeton University Press.

Conversi, Daniele (1997): *The Basques, the Catalans and Spain: Alternative Routes to Nationalist Mobilisation*. London: C. Hurst and Co.

Corrigan, Philip and Sayer, Derek (1985): *The Great Arch: English State Formation as Cultural Revolution*. Oxford: Blackwell.

Cottam, Richard (1979): *Nationalism in Iran*. Pittsburgh, PA: Pittsburgh University Press.

Crow, Tom (1985): *Painters and Public Life in Eighteenth Century Paris*. New Haven and London: Yale University Press.

David, Rosalie (1982): *The Ancient Egyptians: Beliefs and Practices*. London and Boston: Routledge and Kegan Paul.

Delanty, Gerard (1995): *Inventing Europe: Idea, Identity, Reality*. Basingstoke: Macmillan.

De Paor, Liam (1986): *The Peoples of Ireland*. London: Hutchinson and Co. Ltd, and Notre Dame, IN: University of Notre Dame Press.

Deutsch, Karl (1966): *Nationalism and Social Communications*, 2nd edn. New York: MIT Press.

Deutsch, Karl and Foltz, William (eds) (1963): *Nation-Building*. New York: Atherton.

Diaz-Andreu, Margarita and Champion, Timothy (eds) (1996): *Nationalism and Archaeology in Europe*. London: UCL Press.

Diaz-Andreu, Margarita and Smith, Anthony D. (eds) (2001): 'Nationalism and Archaeology', *Nations and Nationalism* 7, 4 (special issue).

Dieckhoff, Alain (2000): *La Nation dans tous ses états: Les identités nationales en mouvement*. Paris: Flammarion.

Doak, Kevin (1997): 'What is a nation and who belongs? National narratives and the ethnic imagination in twentieth-century Japan'. *American Historical Review* 102, 2: 282–309.

Dunn, John (1978): *Western Political Theory in the Face of the Future*. Cambridge: Cambridge University Press.

Durkheim, Emile (1915): *The Elementary Forms of the Religious Life*, trans. J. Swain. London: Allen and Unwin.

Elazar, David (1986): 'The Jewish people as the classic diaspora: A political analysis', in Gabriel Sheffer (ed.), *Modern Diasporas in International Politics*. London and Sydney: Croom Helm.

Eley, Geoff and Suny, Ronald (eds) (1996): *Becoming National*. New York and London: Oxford University Press.

Eller, Jack and Coughlan, Reed (1993): 'The poverty of primordialism: the demystification of ethnic attachments'. *Ethnic and Racial Studies* 16, 2: 183–202.

Eriksen, Thomas Hylland (1993): *Ethnicity and Nationalism*. London and Boulder, CO: Pluto Press.

Esman, Milton (ed.) (1977): *Ethnic Conflict in the Western World*. Ithaca, NY: Cornell University Press.

Esman, Milton (1994): *Ethnic Politics*. Ithaca and London: Cornell University Press.

Featherstone, Mike (ed.) (1990): *Global Culture: Nationalism, Globalisation and Modernity*. London, Newbury Park, and New Delhi: Sage Publications.

Finley, Moses (1986): *The Use and Abuse of History*. London: Hogarth Press.

Fishman, Joshua (1980): 'Social theory and ethnography: neglected perspectives on language and ethnicity in Eastern Europe', in Peter Sugar (ed.), *Ethnic Diversity and Conflict in Eastern Europe*. Santa Barbara: ABC-Clio.

Fondation Hardt (1962): *Grecs et Barbares: Entretiens sur l'Antiquité Classique* VIII, Geneva.

Frankfort, Henri (1948): *Kingship and the Gods*. Chicago: Chicago University Press.

Freeden, Michael (1998): 'Is nationalism a distinct ideology?'. *Political Studies* XLVI: 748–65.

Frye, Richard (1966): *The Heritage of Persia*. New York: Mentor.

Frye, Richard (1975): *The Golden Age of Persia: The Arabs in the East*. London: Weidenfeld and Nicolson.

Gans, Herbert (1979): 'Symbolic ethnicity'. *Ethnic and Racial Studies* 2, 1: 1–20.

Geertz, Clifford (1973): *The Interpretation of Cultures*. London: Fontana.

Gellner, Ernest (1964): *Thought and Change*. London: Weidenfeld and Nicolson.

Gellner, Ernest (1973): 'Scale and Nation'. *Philosophy of the Social Sciences* 3: 1–17.

Gellner, Ernest (1983): *Nations and Nationalism*. Oxford: Blackwell.

Gellner, Ernest (1996): 'Do nations have navels?'. *Nations and Nationalism* 2, 3: 366–70.

Gellner, Ernest (1997): *Nationalism*, London: Weidenfeld and Nicolson.

Gershoni, Israel and Jankowski, Mark (1987): *Egypt, Islam and the Arabs: The Search for Egyptian Nationhood, 1900–1930*. New York and Oxford: Oxford University Press.

Giddens, Anthony (1985): *The Nation-State and Violence*. Cambridge: Polity.

Giddens, Anthony (1991): *The Conditions of Modernity*. Cambridge: Polity.

Gilbert, Paul (1998): *The Philosophy of Nationalism*. Boulder, CO: Westview Press.

Gildea, Robert (1994): *The Past in French History*. New Haven, CT, and London: Yale University Press.

Gillingham, John (1992): 'The beginnings of English imperialism'. *Journal of Historical Sociology* 5, 4: 392–409.

Gillis, John (ed.) (1994): *Commemorations: The Politics of National Identity*. Princeton: Princeton University Press.

Glazer, Nathan and Moynihan, Daniel (eds) (1963): *Beyond the Melting-Pot*. Cambridge, MA: MIT Press.

Glazer, Nathan and Moynihan, Daniel (eds) (1975): *Ethnicity: Theory and Experience*, Cambridge, MA: Harvard University Press.

Glenny, Misha (1990): *The Rebirth of History*. Harmondsworth: Penguin.

Goldberg, Harvey (ed.) (1996): *Sephardi and Middle Eastern Jewries: History and Culture in the Modern Era*. Bloomington, IN: Indiana University Press.

Greenfeld, Liah (1992): *Nationalism: Five Roads to Modernity*. Cambridge, MA: Harvard University Press.

Grosby, Steven (1991): 'Religion and nationality in antiquity'. *European Journal of Sociology* 32: 229–65.

Grosby, Steven (1994): 'The verdict of history: the inexpungeable tie of primordiality – a reply to Eller and Coughlan'. *Ethnic and Racial Studies* 17, 1: 164–71.

Grosby, Steven (1995): 'Territoriality: the transcendental, primordial feature of modern societies'. *Nations and Nationalism* 1, 2: 143–62.

Grosby, Steven (1997): 'Borders, territory and nationality in the ancient Near East and Armenia'. *Journal of the Economic and Social History of the Orient* 40, 1: 1–29.

Guibernau, Monserrat (1996): *Nationalisms: The Nation-state and Nationalism in the Twentieth Century*. Cambridge: Polity.

Guibernau, Monserrat (1999): *Nations without States: Political Communities in a Global Age*. Cambridge: Polity.

Gutierrez, Natividad (1999): *The Culture of the Nation: The Ethnic Nation and Official Nationalism in Twentieth-Century Mexico*. Lincoln, NB: University of Nebraska Press.

Hall, John (ed.) (1998): *The State of the Nation; Ernest Gellner and the Theory of Nationalism*. Cambridge: Cambridge University Press.

Hall, Stuart (1992): 'The new ethnicities', in J. Donald and A. Rattansi (eds), *Race, Culture and Difference*. London: Sage.

Harvey, David (1989): *The Conditions of Postmodernity*. Oxford: Blackwell.

Hastings, Adrian (1997): *The Construction of Nationhood: Ethnicity, Religion and Nationalism*. Cambridge: Cambridge University Press.

Hayes, Carlton (1931): *The Historical Evolution of Modern Nationalism*. New York: Smith.

Hechter, Michael (1975): *Internal Colonialism: The Celtic Fringe in British National Development, 1536–1966*. London: Routledge and Kegan Paul.

Hechter, Michael (1988): 'Rational choice theory and the study of ethnic and race relations', in John Rex and David Mason (eds), *Theories of Ethnic and Race Relations*. Cambridge: Cambridge University Press.

Hechter, Michael (1992): 'The dynamics of secession'. *Acta Sociologica* 35: 267–83.

Hechter, Michael (1995): 'Explaining nationalist violence'. *Nations and Nationalism* 1, 1: 53–68.

Hechter, Michael (2000): *Containing Nationalism*. Oxford and New York: Oxford University Press.

Hedetoft, Ulf (1995): *Signs of Nations: Studies in the Political Semiotics of Self and Other in Contemporary European Nationalism*. Aldershot: Dartmouth Publishing Company.

Herb, Guntram and Kaplan, David (eds) (1999): *Nested Identities: Nationalism, Territory and Scale*. Lanham, Maryland: Rowman and Littlefield Publishers.

Herberg, Will (1960): *Protestant–Catholic–Jew*. New York: Doubleday.

Herbert, Robert (1972): *David, Voltaire, Brutus and the French Revolution*. London: Allen Lane.

Herder, Johann Gottfried (1877–1913): *Sämmtliche Werke*, ed. B. Suphan. Berlin: Weidmann.

Hobsbawm, Eric (1990): *Nations and Nationalism since 1780*. Cambridge: Cambridge University Press.

Hobsbawm, Eric and Ranger, Terence (eds) (1983): *The Invention of Tradition*. Cambridge: Cambridge University Press.

Hooson, David (ed.) (1994): *Geography and National Identity*. Oxford: Blackwell.

Horowitz, Donald (1985): *Ethnic Groups in Conflict*. Berkeley and Los Angeles: University of California Press.

Horowitz, Donald (1992): 'Irredentas and secessions: adjacent phenomena, neglected connections', in A. D. Smith (ed.), *Ethnicity and Nationalism: International Studies in Sociology and Social Anthropology*, vol. LX. Leiden: Brill.

Hosking, Geoffrey and Schöpflin, George (eds) (1997): *Myths and Nationhood*. London and New York: Routledge.

Hroch, Miroslav (1985): *Social Preconditions of National Revival in Europe*. Cambridge: Cambridge University Press.

Humphreys, R. A. and Lynch, J. (eds) (1965): *The Origins of the Latin American Revolutions, 1808–25*. New York: Knopf.

Hutchinson, John (1987): *The Dynamics of Cultural Nationalism: The Gaelic Revival and the Creation of the Irish Nation State*. London: Allen and Unwin.

Hutchinson, John (1994): *Modern Nationalism*. London: Fontana.

Hutchinson, John (2000): 'Ethnicity and modern nations'. *Ethnic and Racial Studies* 23, 4: 651–69.

Ichijo, Atsuko (1998): 'Scottish Nationalism and Identity in the Age of European Integration', unpublished Ph.D. thesis. University of London.

Im Hof, Ulrich (1991): *Mythos-Schweiz: Identität-Nation-Geschichte*. Zürich: Neue Verlag Zürcher Zeitung.

Jones, Sian (1997): *The Archaeology of Ethnicity: Constructing Identities in the Past and the Present*. London and New York: Routledge.

Juergensmeyer, Mark (1993): *The New Cold War? Religious Nationalism Confronts the Secular State*. Berkeley and Los Angeles: University of California Press.

Just, Roger (1989): 'The triumph of the *ethnos*', in Elisabeth Tonkin, Maryon McDonald and Malcolm Chapman (eds), *History and Ethnicity*. London and New York: Routledge.

Kahan, Arcadius (1968): 'Nineteenth-century European experience with policies of economic nationalism', in H. G. Johnson (ed.), *Economic Nationalism in Old and New States*. London: Allen and Unwin.

Kaldor, Mary (1999): *New and Old Wars: Organized Violence in a Global Era*. Cambridge: Polity.

Kandiyoti, Deniz (ed.) (2000): 'Gender and Nationalism'. *Nations and Nationalism* 6, 4 (special issue).

Kapferer, Bruce (1988): *Legends of People, Myths of State: Violence, Intolerance and Political Culture in Sri Lanka and Australia*. Washington, DC, and London: Smithsonian Institution Press.

Kaufman, Eric and Zimmer, Oliver (1998): 'In search of the authentic nation: Landscape and national identity in Switzerland and Canada'. *Nations and Nationalism* 4, 4: 483–510.

Kautsky, John (ed.) (1962): *Political Change in Underdeveloped Countries*. New York: John Wiley.

Kearney, Hugh (1990): *The British Isles, A History of Four Nations*. Cambridge: Cambridge University Press.

Keddie, Nikki (1981): *Roots of Revolution: An Interpretive History of Modern Iran*. New Haven, CT: Yale University Press.

Kedourie, Elie (1960): *Nationalism*. London: Hutchinson.

Kedourie, Elie (ed.) (1971): *Nationalism in Asia and Africa*. London: Weidenfeld and Nicolson.

Kedourie, Elie (ed.) (1992): *Spain and the Jews: The Sephardi Experience, 1492 and After*. London: Thames and Hudson Ltd.

Kedward, Roderick (ed.) (1965): *The Dreyfus Affair*. London: Longman.

Kemilainen, Aira (1964): *Nationalism, Problems concerning the Word, the Concept and Classification*. Yvaskyla: Kustantajat Publishers.

Kennedy, Emmet (1989): *A Cultural History of the French Revolution*. New Haven, CT, and London: Yale University Press.

Kenrick, Donald and Puxon, Graham (1972): *The Destiny of Europe's Gypsies*. London: Chatto-Heinemann.

Kidd, Colin (1999): *British Identities before Nationalism: Ethnicity and Nationhood in the Atlantic World, 1600–1800*. Cambridge: Cambridge University Press.

Kitromilides, Paschalis (1989): ' "Imagined communities" and the origins of the national question in the Balkans'. *European History Quarterly* 19, 2: 149–92.

Kitromilides, Paschalis (1998): 'On the intellectual content of Greek nationalism: Paparrigopoulos, Byzantium and the Great Idea', in David Ricks and Paul Magdalino (eds), *Byzantium and the Modern Greek Identity*. King's College London: Centre for Hellenic Studies. Aldershot: Ashgate Publishing.

Knoll, Paul (1993): 'National consciousness in medieval Poland', *Ethnic Studies* 10, 1: 65–84.

Kohl, Philip and Fawcett, Clare (eds) (1995): *Nationalism, Politics and the Practice of Archaeology*. Cambridge: Cambridge University Press.

Kohn, Hans (1940): 'The origins of English nationalism'. *Journal of the History of Ideas* I: 69–94.

Kohn, Hans (1955): *Nationalism, Its Meaning and History*. New York: Van Nostrand.

Kohn, Hans (1965): *The Mind of Germany*. London: Macmillan.

Kohn, Hans (1967a): *The Idea of Nationalism* [1944], 2nd edn. New York: Collier-Macmillan.

Kohn, Hans (1967b): *Prelude to Nation-States: The French and German Experience, 1789–1815*. New York: Van Nostrand.

Kreis, Jacob (1991): *Der Mythos von 1291: Zur Enstehung des Schweizerischen Nationalfeiertags*. Basel: Friedrich Reinhardt Verlag.

Lang, David (1980): *Armenia, Cradle of Civilisation*. London: Allen and Unwin.

Lartichaux, J.-Y. (1977): 'Linguistic Politics during the French Revolution'. *Diogenes* 97: 65–84.

Lehmann, Jean-Pierre (1982): *The Roots of Modern Japan*. London and Basingstoke: Macmillan.

Leifer, Michael (ed.) (2000): *Asian Nationalism*. Routledge: London and New York.

Llobera, Josep (1994): *The God of Modernity*. Oxford: Berg.

Lydon, James (1995): 'Nation and race in medieval Ireland', in Simon Forde, Lesley Johnson and Alan Murray (eds), *Concepts of National Identity in the Middle Ages*. Leeds: University of Leeds: Leeds Studies in English.

Lyons, F. S. (1979): *Culture and Anarchy in Ireland, 1890–1930*. London: Oxford University Press.

Mann, Michael (1993): *The Sources of Social Power*, vol. II. Cambridge: Cambridge University Press.

Mann, Michael (1995): 'A political theory of nationalism and its excesses', in Sukumar Periwal (ed.), *Notions of Nationalism*. Budapest: Central European University Press.

Marwick, Arthur (1974): *War and Social Change in the Twentieth Century*. London: Methuen.

Matossian, Mary (1962): 'Ideologies of "delayed industrialization": Some tensions and ambiguities', in John Kautsky (ed.), *Political Change in Underdeveloped Countries*. New York: John Wiley.

Mayall, James (1990): *Nationalism and International Society*. Cambridge: Cambridge University Press.

McCrone, David (1998): *The Sociology of Nationalism*. London and New York: Routledge.

McNeill, William (1986): *Polyethnicity and National Unity in World History*. Toronto: University of Toronto Press.

Melucci, Alberto (1989): *Nomads of the Present: Social Movements and Individual Needs in Contemporary Society*. London: Hutchinson Radius.

Mendels, Doron (1992): *The Rise and Fall of Jewish Nationalism*. New York: Doubleday.

Michelat, G. and Thomas, J.-P. H. (1966): *Dimensions du nationalisme*. Paris: Librairie Armand Colin.

Miller, David (1995): *On Nationality*. Oxford: Oxford University Press.

Minogue, Kenneth (1967): *Nationalism*. London: Batsford.

Mitchell, Marion (1931): 'Emile Durkheim and the philosophy of nationalism'. *Political Science Quarterly* 46: 87–106.

Mosse, George (1964): *The Crisis of German Ideology*. New York: Grosset and Dunlap.

Mosse, George (1975): *The Nationalization of the Masses: Political Symbolism and Mass Movements in Germany from the Napoleonic Wars through the Third Reich*. Ithaca, NY: Cornell University Press.

Mosse, George (1990): *Fallen Soldiers*. Oxford and New York: Oxford University Press.

Mosse, George (1994): *Confronting the Nation: Jewish and Western Nationalism*. Hanover, NH: University Press of New England/Brandeis University.

Motyl, Alexander (1999): *Revolutions, Nations, Empires*. New York: Columbia University Press.

Nairn, Tom (1977): *The Break-up of Britain: Crisis and Neo-Nationalism*. London: Verso.

Nairn, Tom (1997): *Faces of Nationalism: Janus Revisited*. London: Verso.

Nash, Manning (1989): *The Cauldron of Ethnicity in the Modern World*. Chicago, IL. and London: University of Chicago Press.

Nora, Pierre (1997–8): *Realms of Memory: The Construction of the French Past*, ed. Lawrence Kritzman. New York: Columbia University Press, 3 vols (orig. *Les Lieux de memoire*, Paris: Gallimard, 7 vols, 1984–92).

O'Brien, Conor Cruse (1988a): *God-Land: Reflections on Religion and Nationalism*. Cambridge, MA: Harvard University Press.

O'Brien, Conor Cruse (1988b): 'Nationalism and the French Revolution', in Geoffrey Best (ed.), *The Permanent Revolution: The French Revolution and Its Legacy, 1789–1989*. London: Fontana.

Okamura, J. (1981): 'Situational ethnicity'. *Ethnic and Racial Studies* 4, 4: 452–65.

O'Leary, Brendan (ed.) (1996): 'Symposium on David Miller's *On Nationality*'. *Nations and Nationalism* 2, 3: 409–51.

O'Leary, Brendan (1998): 'Ernest Gellner's diagnoses of nationalism: or, what is living and what is dead in Ernest Gellner's philosophy of nationalism?', in John Hall (ed.), *The State of the Nation: Ernest Gellner and the Theory of Nationalism*. Cambridge: Cambridge University Press.

Orridge, Andrew (1982): 'Separatist and autonomist nationalisms: the structure of regional loyalties in the modern state', in Colin Williams (ed.), *National Separatism*. Cardiff: University of Wales Press.

Panossian, Razmik (2000): 'The Evolution of Multilocal National Identity and the Contemporary Politics of Nationalism: Armenia and Its Diaspora', unpublished Ph.D. thesis. University of London.

Parekh, Bikhu (1995): 'Ethnocentricity of the nationalist discourse'. *Nations and Nationalism* 1, 1: 25–52.

Parsons, Talcott (1966): *Societies, Evolutionary and Comparative Perspectives*. Englewood Cliffs: Prentice-Hall.

Pearson, Raymond (1993): 'Fact, fantasy, fraud: perceptions and projections of national revival', *Ethnic Groups* 10, 1–3; 43–64.

Peel, John (1989): 'The cultural work of Yoruba ethno-genesis', in Elisabeth Tonkin, Maryon McDonald and Malcolm Chapman (eds), *History and Ethnicity*. London and New York: Routledge.

Penrose, Jan (1995): 'Essential constructions? The "cultural bases" of nationalist movements', *Nations and Nationalism* 1, 3: 391–417.

Periwal, Sukumar (ed.) (1995): *Notions of Nationalism*. Budapest: Central European University Press.

Petersen, William (1975): 'On the sub-nations of Europe', in Nathan Glazer and Daniel Moynihan (eds), *Ethnicity: Theory and Experience*. Cambridge, MA: Harvard University Press.

Pieterse, Neederveen (1995): 'Europe among other things: closure, culture, identity', in K. von Benda-Beckmann and M. Verkuyten (eds), *Nationalism, Ethnicity and Cultural Identity in Europe*. Utrecht: ERCOMER.

Plamenatz, John (1976): 'Two types of nationalism', in Eugene Kamenka (ed.), *Nationalism: The Nature and Evolution of an Idea*. London: Edward Arnold.

Poole, Ross (1999): *Nation and Identity*. London and New York: Routledge.

Preece, Jennifer Jackson (1998): *National Minorities and the European Nation-States System*. Oxford: Clarendon Press.

Purvis, James (1968): *The Samaritan Pentateuch and the Origins of the Samaritan Sect*, Harvard Semitic Monographs, vol. 2. Cambridge, MA: Harvard University Press.

Ram, Uri (1995): 'Zionist historiography and the invention of Jewish nationhood: The case of Ben-Zion Dinur'. *History and Memory* 7: 91–124.

Ram, Uri (1998): 'Postnationalist pasts: The case of Israel'. *Social Science History* 22, 4: 513–45.

Ramet, Sabrina (1996): *Balkan Babel: The Disintegration of Yugoslavia from the Death of Tito to Ethnic War*, 2nd edn. Boulder, CO: Westview Press.

Renan, Ernest (1882): *Qu'est-ce qu'une nation?*. Paris: Calmann-Levy.

Reynolds, Susan (1984): *Kingdoms and Communities in Western Europe, 900–1300*. Oxford: Clarendon Press.

Richmond, Anthony (1984): 'Ethnic nationalism and post-industrialism'. *Ethnic and Racial Studies* 7, 1: 4–18.

Riekmann, Sonja Puntscher (1997): 'The myth of European unity', in Geoffrey Hosking and George Schöpflin (eds), *Myths and Nationhood*. London and New York: Routledge.

Roberts, Michael (1993): 'Nationalism, the past and the present: the case of Sri Lanka'. *Ethnic and Racial Studies* 16, 1: 133–66.

Robinson, Francis (1979): 'Islam and Muslim separatism', in David Taylor and Malcolm Yapp (eds), *Political Identity in South Asia*. Dublin and London: Curzon Press.

Rosdolsky, R. (1964): 'Friedrich Engels und das Problem der "Geschichtslosen Völker"'. *Archiv für Sozialgeschichte* 4: 87–282.

Rotberg, Robert (1967): 'African nationalism: concept or confusion?'. *Journal of Modern African Studies* 4, 1: 33–46.

Roudometov, Victor (1998): 'From "*Rum millet*" to Greek nation: Enlightenment, secularisation and national identity in Ottoman Balkan society, 1453–1821'. *Journal of Modern Greek Studies* 16, 1: 11–48.

Rousseau, Jean-Jacques (1915): *The Political Writings of Rousseau*, 2 vols, ed. C. E. Vaughan. Cambridge: Cambridge University Press.

Roux, Georges (1964): *Ancient Iraq*. Harmondsworth: Penguin.

Rustow, Dankwart (1967): *A World of Nations*. Washington DC: Brookings Institution.

Sarkisyanz, Emanuel (1964): *Buddhist Backgrounds of the Burmese Revolution*. The Hague: Nijhoff.

Schama, Simon (1987): *The Embarrassment of Riches: An Interpretation of Dutch Culture in the Golden Age*. London: William Collins.

Schama, Simon (1989): *Citizens: A Chronicle of the French Revolution*. New York: Knopf, and London: Penguin.

Schama, Simon (1995): *Landscape and Memory*. London: Harper Collins (Fontana).

Scheuch, Erwin (1966): 'Cross-national comparisons with aggregate data', in Richard Merritt and Stein Rokkan (eds), *Comparing Nations: The Use of Quantitative Data in Cross-National Research*. New Haven, CT: Yale University Press.

Schlesinger, Philip (1987): 'On national identity: some conceptions and misconceptions criticised'. *Social Science Information* 26, 2: 219–64.

Schlesinger, Philip (1991): *Media, State and Nation: Political Violence and Collective Identities*. London: Sage.

Schlesinger, Philip (1992): 'Europe – a new cultural battlefield?'. *Innovation* 5, 1: 11–23.

Schnapper, Dominique (1997): 'Beyond the opposition: "civic" nation versus "ethnic" nation'. *ASEN Bulletin* 12: 4–8.

Schöpflin, George (2000): *Nations, Identity, Power: The New Politics of Europe*. London: C. Hurst and Co.

Schulze, Hagen (1996): *States, Nations and Nationalism*. Oxford: Blackwell.

Scott, George Jnr (1990): 'A resynthesis of primordial and circumstantialist approaches to ethnic group solidarity: towards an explanatory model'. *Ethnic and Racial Studies* 13, 2: 148–71.

Seltzer, Robert (1980): *Jewish People, Jewish Thought*. New York: Macmillan.

Seton-Watson (1977): *Nations and States*. London: Methuen.

Sheffer, Gabriel (ed.) (1986): *Modern Diasporas in International Politics*. London and Sydney: Croom Helm.

Shils, Edward (1957): 'Primordial, personal, sacred and civil ties'. *British Journal of Sociology* 7: 13–45.

Sluga, Glenda (1998): 'Identity, gender and the history of European nations and nationalism'. *Nations and Nationalism* 4, 1: 87–111.

Smith, Anthony D. (1979): *Nationalism in the Twentieth Century*. Oxford: Martin Robertson.

Smith, Anthony D. (1981a): *The Ethnic Revival in the Modern World*. Cambridge: Cambridge University Press.

Smith, Anthony D. (1981b): 'War and ethnicity: the role of warfare in the formation of self-images and cohesion of ethnic communities'. *Ethnic and Racial Studies* 4, 4: 375–97.

Smith, Anthony D. (1983): *Theories of Nationalism*, 2nd edn. London: Duckworth, and New York: Holmes and Meier.

Smith, Anthony D. (1986): *The Ethnic Origins of Nations*. Oxford: Blackwell.

Smith, Anthony D. (1989): 'The origins of nations'. *Ethnic and Racial Studies* 12, 3: 340–67.

Smith, Anthony D. (1991): *National Identity*. Harmondsworth: Penguin.

Smith, Anthony D. (1992): 'National identity and the idea of European unity'. *International Affairs* 68, 1: 55–76.

Smith, Anthony D. (1994): 'The problem of national identity: ancient, medieval, modern?'. *Ethnic and Racial Studies* 17, 3: 375–99.

Smith, Anthony D. (1995): *Nations and Nationalism in a Global Era*. Cambridge: Polity.

Smith, Anthony D. (1997): 'The Golden Age and national renewal', in Geoffrey Hosking and George Schöpflin (eds), *Myths and Nationhood*. London: Routledge.

Smith, Anthony D. (1998): *Nationalism and Modernism*. London and New York: Routledge.

Smith, Anthony D. (1999a): *Myths and Memories of the Nation*. Oxford and New York: Oxford University Press.

Smith, Anthony D. (1999b): 'Sacred territories and national conflict'. *Israel Affairs* 5, 4: 13–31.

Smith, Anthony D. (2000a): *The Nation in History*. Hanover, NH: University Press of New England/Brandeis University, and Cambridge: Polity.

Smith, Anthony D. (2000b): 'The "Sacred" dimension of nationalism'. *Millennium: Journal of International Politics* 29, 3: 791–814.

Smith, D. E. (ed.) (1974): *Religion and Political Modernization*. New Haven, CT: Yale University Press.

Snyder, Louis (1954): *The Meaning of Nationalism*. New Brunswick: Rutgers University Press.

Snyder, Louis (1976): *The Varieties of Nationalism: A Comparative View*. Hinsdale, Illinois: The Dryden Press.

Soysal, Yacemin (1994): *Limits of Citizenship: Migrants and Post-national Membership in Europe*. Chicago, IL: University of Chicago Press.

Stack, John (ed.) (1986): *The Primordial Challenge: Ethnicity in the Contemporary World*. New York: Greenwood Press.

Stalin, Joseph (1973): 'The Nation', in idem, *Marxism and the National Question*, reprinted in Bruce Franklin (ed.), *The Essential Stalin: Major Theoretical Writings, 1905–52*. London: Croom Helm.

Steinberg, Jonathan (1976): *Why Switzerland?*. Cambridge: Cambridge University Press.

Stern, Menahem (1972): 'The Hasmonean revolt and its place in the history of Jewish society and religion', in Haim Ben-Sasson and Shmuel Ettinger (eds), *Jewish Society Through the Ages*. New York: Schocken Books.

Stone, John (ed.) (1979): 'Internal Colonialism'. *Ethnic and Racial Studies* 2, 3 (special issue).

Subaratnam, Lakshmanan (1997): 'Motifs, metaphors and mytho-moteurs: some reflections on medieval South Asian ethnicity'. *Nations and Nationalism* 3, 3: 397–426.

Subtelny, Orest (1994): *Ukraine: A History*, 2nd edn. Toronto, Buffalo, London: University of Toronto Press.

Sugar, Peter (ed.) (1980): *Ethnic Diversity and Conflict in Eastern Europe*. Santa Barbara: ABC-Clio.

Suny, Ronald (1993): *The Revenge of the Past: Nationalism, Revolution and the Collapse of the Soviet Union*. Stanford, CA: Stanford University Press.

Tilly, Charles (ed.) (1975): *The Formation of National States in Western Europe*. Princeton: Princeton University Press.

Tomlinson, John (1991): *Cultural Imperialism*. London: Pinter Publishers.

Tonkin, Elisabeth, McDonald, Maryon and Chapman, Malcolm (eds) (1989): *History and Ethnicity*. London and New York: Routledge.

Tønnesson, Stein and Antlov, Hans (eds) (1996): *Asian Forms of the Nation*. Cambridge: Cambridge University Press.

Trevor-Roper, Hugh (1961): *Jewish and Other Nationalisms*. London: Weidenfeld and Nicolson.

Trigger, B. G., Kemp, B. J., O'Connor, D. and Lloyd, A. B. (1983): *Egypt: A Social History*. Cambridge: Cambridge University Press.

Tuveson, E. L. (1968): *Redeemer Nation: The Idea of America's Millennial Role*. Chicago: Chicago University Press.

Van den Berghe, Pierre (1978): 'Race and ethnicity: a sociobiological perspective'. *Ethnic and Racial Studies* 1, 4: 401–11.

Van den Berghe, Pierre (1995): 'Does race matter?'. *Nations and Nationalism* 1, 3: 357–68.

Van der Veer, Peter (1994): *Religious Nationalisms: Hindus and Muslims in India*. Berkeley, CA: University of California Press.

Viroli, Maurizio (1995): *For Love of Country: An Essay on Nationalism and Patriotism*. Oxford: Clarendon Press.

Vital, David (1975): *The Origins of Zionism*. Oxford: Clarendon.

Vital, David (1990): *The Future of the Jews: A People at the Crossroads?*. Cambridge, MA, and London: Harvard University Press.

Wallace, William (1990): *The Transformation of Western Europe*. London: RIIA/Pinter.

Walzer, Michael (1985): *Exodus and Revolution*. New York: Basic Books.

Weber, Eugene (1979): *Peasants into Frenchmen: The Modernisation of Rural France, 1870–1914*. London: Chatto and Windus.

Weber, Eugene (1991): *My France: Politics, Culture, Myth*. Cambridge, MA: Harvard University Press.

Weber, Max (1948): *From Max Weber: Essays in Sociology*, ed. Hans Gerth and C. Wright Mills. London: Routledge and Kegan Paul.

Weber, Max (1968): *Economy and Society*, 3 vols. New York: Bedminster Press.

Webster, Bruce (1997): *Medieval Scotland: The Making of an Identity*. Basingstoke: The Macmillan Press.

Wiberg, Hakan (1983): 'Self-determination as an international issue', in Ioann Lewis (ed.), *Nationalism and Self-Determination in the Horn of Africa*. London: Ithaca Press.

Williams, Gwyn (1985): *When was Wales?*. Harmondsworth: Penguin.

Wilmsen, Edwin and McAllister, Patrick (eds) (1996): *The Politics of Difference: Ethnic Premises in a World of Power*. Chicago, IL, and London: University of Chicago Press.

Wilson, H. S. (ed.) (1969): *Origins of West African Nationalism*. London: Macmillan and Co.

Winter, Jay (1995): *Sites of Memory, Sites of Mourning*. Cambridge: Cambridge University Press.

Wiseman, D. J. (ed.) (1973): *Peoples of the Old Testament*. Oxford: Clarendon Press.

Wright, John, Goldenberg, Suzanne and Schofield, Richard (eds) (1996): *Transcaucasian Boundaries*. London: UCL Press.

Yuval-Davis, Nira (1997): *Gender and Nation*. London: Sage.

Yuval-Davis, Nira and Anthias, Floya (eds) (1989): *Woman-Nation-State*. London: Sage.

Zartmann, William (1964): *Government and Politics in North Africa*. New York: Praeger.

Zeitlin, Irving (1984): *Ancient Judaism*. Cambridge: Polity.

Zernatto, Guido (1944): 'Nation: the history of a word'. *Review of Politics* 6: 351–66.

Zerubavel, Yael (1995): *Recovered Roots: Collective Memory and the Making of Israeli National Tradition*. Chicago, IL, and London: University of Chicago Press.

Zimmer, Oliver (1999): 'Forging the Swiss Nation, 1760–1939: Popular Memory, Patriotic Invention and Competing Conceptions of Nationhood', unpublished Ph.D. thesis. University of London.

Index

Page references in *italics* indicate a significant section on a particular subject in the text.